What readers have been saying about *The Enemy Within:*

"The great but cumbersome Puritan John Owen has long been helping Christians to detect indwelling sin, a.k.a. the flesh, in themselves and to overcome it by divine power. Kris Lundgaard presents Owen's teaching on the battle with sin—no more, no less—unshelled and up-dated for today's readers, with questions to help us take it to heart. This book will surely be a milestone for many in the present, just as the original Owen was for many in the past. I heartily commend what Lundgaard has done."

J. I. Packer
Regent College

"John Owen's treatises on *Indwelling Sin in Believers* and *The Mortification of Sin* are, in my opinion, the most helpful writings on personal holiness ever written. Yet his ponderous, seventeenth-century style is too much for most of today's readers. In *The Enemy Within: Straight Talk About the Power and Defeat of Sin*, Kris Lundgaard has done a notable job of making Owen's teaching readable once again. This is not a twentieth-century revision of Owen, but a fresh, contemporary, highly readable book written in Lundgaard's own style, yet remarkably true to Owen's teaching. Every Christian who is serious about holiness should read this book."

Jerry Bridges
The Navigators

"Kris Lundgaard has done the impossible. He has given us some of the best of Puritan theology in language all of us can understand. But watch out. His penetrating style as he exposes sin's deceit will challenge you to radical spiritual transformation! What a wonderful experience to read such a fine author. We can only hope he will give us more."

Richard L. Pratt, Jr.
Reformed Theological Seminary

"Kris Lundgaard has given us a delightful book. Most books about sin don't take God's holiness very seriously or take my lack of it so seriously I can't deal with the guilt. This book does neither. It is honest, real, and, best of all, hopeful. I'm going to get better and this book is going to help. Read it. You'll be glad."

Steve Brown
Reformed Theological Seminary

"An able defender of the Reformed faith, Kris Lundgaard presents a thorough and well-articulated battle plan for taking up arms against the flesh. Confronting and overcoming sin is a constant struggle for every believer. Here is a must read for all who desire not to wave the white flag and surrender to sin, but to soundly defeat it."

Steven J. Lawson
Pastor, Dauphin Way Baptist Church

"A remarkable reconnaissance mission behind enemy lines, well describing the spiritual forces that both attack us and attract us by invading our own hearts. Lundgaard forearms us against these assaults by reminding us of how vulnerable we can be when we convince ourselves that we are too secure to fall. Here is a solid reminder that apart from the grace of God we are far weaker than we can imagine—but greater is he that is in us than he that is in the world."

Bryan Chapell
President, Covenant Theological Seminary

the *enemy* within

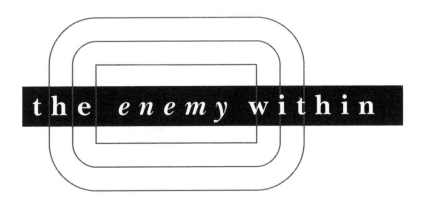

the *enemy* within

STRAIGHT TALK ABOUT THE

POWER AND DEFEAT OF SIN

Kris Lundgaard

PUBLISHING
P.O. BOX 817 • PHILLIPSBURG • NEW JERSEY 08865

Unless otherwise indicated, Scripture quotations are from the HOLY BIBLE, NEW INTERNATIONAL VERSION. Copyright © 1973, 1978, 1984 International Bible Society. Used by permission of Zondervan Bible Publishers. Italics indicate emphasis added.

Page design by Tobias Design
Typesetting by Michelle Feaster

Printed in the United States of America

Library of Congress Cataloging-in-Publication Data
Lundgaard, Kris, 1958–
     The enemy within : straight talk about the power and defeat of sin / Kris Lundgaard.
          p. cm.
     Includes bibliographical references.
     ISBN-10: 0-87552-201-7 (paper)
     ISBN-13: 978-0-87552-201-2 (paper)
     1. Sin. I. Title.
BT715.L86 1998
241'.3—dc21   98–45082

To Nicholas,
my son,
for victory!

contents

preface

"If God has redeemed me from sin, and given me his Holy Spirit to sanctify me and give me strength against sin, why do I go on sinning?" This question has plagued me throughout my life of faith. In my lowest moments it has brought despair; it has even darkened the edges of my brightest times.

In the late summer of 1996 I stumbled across something helpful, something that has given me hope. The name John Owen kept popping up over the years, especially when I read J. I. Packer's books.[1] I steered clear of Owen because I knew from a few forays into his books in seminary that the going would be slow and hard. But when the impotence of my sanctification became glaringly clear to me, every obstacle was overcome, and I picked up my dusty copy of *The Nature, Power, Deceit, and Prevalency of the Remainders of Indwelling Sin in Believers.*[2]

Over the next few weeks I wrestled my way through Owen's cumbersome syntax and antiquated vocabulary, taking an hour to put eight or ten pages behind me. I was reading every sentence two, three, or four times, looking up every Bible reference, thumbing through my dictionary to find "aversation" and "inadvertency," and underlining 80 percent of what I read. It was for my mind the back-breaking work of digging a mine with a pickaxe. But there was gold along the way—not just a handful of dust, but a mother-lode-full of nuggets.

The gold I found was hope, renewed love for Christ, an approach to holiness by faith in him. Along the way I was sick to my stomach over my sin, yet somehow lifted up to the cross for deliverance. When I finished *Indwelling Sin*, I didn't miss a beat, but drove my pick into *The Mortification of Sin*. By now the whole way I looked at holiness was changing, and I believed that by God's grace, looking into the face of Christ to see his glory, I could resist sin to the point of shedding my blood (Hebrews 12:1–4).

My heart wants to share this hope. Over and over in small groups and discipling conversations I have heard my own anguished question ("Why do I still sin?") from the lips of friends. I know John Owen's unfolding of the Scriptures is just what we all need to hear. But I know also that few will ever trouble themselves to hack through his ponderous prose, no matter how passionately I recommend him. The trip back to the seventeenth century is too far. So I decided to bring Owen into the twenty-first century.

I kidnapped Owen. By force I took him as my co-author, and together we've written a new book. He brought to the table his precious exposition, outlines, arguments, and illustrations, and I returned to him stories of bone-marrow transplants and torx sockets, and tried to bring his profound understanding of the Bible into our world. I haven't simply abridged him, as others have done.[3] Yet anyone familiar with him would see his ghost haunting my work.

My aim may be expressed in one unretouched sentence from the end of Owen's preface to *The Mortification of Sin:*

I hope I may own in sincerity, that my heart's desire unto God, and the chief design of my life in the station wherein the good providence of God hath placed me, are that mortification and universal holiness may be promoted in my own and in the hearts and ways of others, to the glory of God; that so the gospel of our Lord and Saviour Jesus Christ may be adorned in all things: for the compassing of which end, if this little discourse . . . may in any thing be useful to the least of the saints, it will be looked on as a return of the weak prayers wherewith it is attended by its unworthy author,

Kris Lundgaard

acknowledgments

This book is clearer than it would have been, thanks to guinea pigs Eric Hoxworth, James Lines, Randy Scott, Geof Smith, the University Presbyterian Church senior high youth group, and one patient adult education class (Brea Smith, Mark and Pam Pflieger, Ed Emerick, Scot Horne, Ed and Patty Hughs, Charlene Hoskins, David Smith, and Johnnie Coble).

Paula Lundgaard, Charlene Hoskins, and Ed and Patty Hughs read and reflected, critiqued and encouraged. Dr. Ed Hoskins clarified and corrected my medical illustrations. (I couldn't use John Owen's seventeenth-century medical stories because I don't know what bile and humours are.) Senior Pastor John Pickett argued with me about sanctification till we both knew better what we were talking about.

Editor Thom Notaro at P&R gave the manuscript a close reading and polished it up, while Barbara Lerch gave sparkling encouragement.

J. I. Packer, though he doesn't know me, gets credit for introducing me to Owen in his class on the English Puritans at Reformed Theological Seminary, and through his frequent expositions of Owen in his books.

If John Owen were alive, he'd be tempted to sue me, I stole so much of his material. I'll apologize and thank him when I see him in glory.

We all worked together *soli Deo gloria.*

part one

The Power of Sin in What It Is

We have met the enemy and he is us.

—Pogo

1 | *evil at my elbow*

God strengthen me to bear myself;
That heaviest weight of all to bear,
Inalienable weight of care.
—Christina Rossetti

I Feel the Same Way Too

All I wanted to do was surprise my wife.

Since we had moved into our new house almost a year ago, the refrigerator door handle had been on the wrong side. I had put off moving it because of my clumsiness with mechanical things. But on this Thursday afternoon while my wife was at work, I was set to redeem myself and right the wrong.

I was halfway through the job. I had the refrigerator and freezer doors off and wanted to get them back on soon so nothing would spoil. I was at the pivotal step of swapping the hinges from the right side of the refrigerator to the left, when I realized that each hinge was fastened by two torx screws. Two lousy torx screws. There is only one tool in the universe that can (safely) remove a torx screw: a torx socket.

I didn't have a torx socket.

Right then my three boys decided to move their Traveling Sibling Rivalry Show into the middle of my angst. I lost it. I let them have it, though they didn't deserve it. They stared at me as if I were a monster from Alpha Centauri, while I ranted in an unknown tongue.

In mid-fit I had an out-of-body experience. I saw my contorted red face screaming at my charming boys and knew at once I was doing something evil. So I stopped and asked their forgiveness, right? Wrong. Something had control of me—it was as if an alien had invaded my body and was forcing me to do his bidding. It was long after they had fled from my wrath before I recovered my sanity and my conscience and humbled myself before them in groveling apologies.

I spent the next several days feeling like a whipped puppy. Was I really that wicked? How could I hurt my children like that? Had I done irreparable harm? Would they forgive me? Would God forgive me?

Anything like that ever happen to you?

When I read Romans 7, I am consoled that Paul felt the same way too.[1] He helps me understand my madness and gives me some juicy theological terms for it: "the law of sin" (Romans 7:23), "this body of death" (verse 24), "my sinful nature" ("my flesh" in many translations, verse 18), "sin living in me" (verse 17), just plain "sin" (verse 11), and "the law of sin and death" (8:2). Theologians like to call it "indwelling sin."[2] Whatever we call it, it's an enemy of God and of our souls.[3] The reason for this book is that the first step to fighting this enemy is to know it—and to know it well.

The foundation of our knowledge of the power of indwelling sin in the life of a believer is laid in Paul's own experience. He slugged his way through the fight till, at times, he was on the ropes, crying out from the edge of defeat (Romans 7:23–24). Yet when the bell rang, he stood with his foot on the neck of his enemy, and held up his hand to receive the crown of righteousness (2 Timothy 4:7–8).

Four Key Truths

If we want to stand in conquest over our bleeding flesh, we'll have to follow Paul into the fight. When we do, we'll find the same four truths that humbled him in battle, all expressed in one verse:

> So I find this law at work: When I want to do good, evil is right there with me. (Romans 7:21)

1. Sin living in us is a "law." The "law" Paul refers to is the same thing he calls "sin living in me" in verses 20 and 23. This is the indwelling sin we are talking about. Why call it a *law*?

Paul uses "law" as a metaphor. He needs a way to express the power, authority, constraint, and control that sin wields in our lives, and he picks "law" with a touch of irony. He has been writing earlier in the chapter of *God's* law, which is supposed to rule our lives, yet the law of *sin* seems to win a lot of head-to-head battles. Could he have chosen a more stunning contrast to unmask sin's deadly force?

Chew on the metaphor of law for a minute. We can think of it in one way as a moral rule that directs and commands us to do what it requires ("Honor your parents") or not do what it forbids ("Do not trespass"). More than that, a law entices us to obey with offers of reward ("you will live long in the land") and compels us to submit by threats of punishment for disobedience ("$500 fine for trespassing").

We can also think of law in the way we speak of "laws of nature." Gravity, for example, is a law that bends things in its direction. It perfectly conforms us to its "commands." Gravity is not a law as an idea or an outward precept, but a force that can make objects "obey" its "will." In this sense every urge and inclination in us is a law. Hunger is a law, thirst, sexual drive, fear—each impels us to fulfill its demands, and each brings a force to bear on us to bow us into submission.

Indwelling sin works like this—enticing, threatening, even bullying. So Paul calls it a law to get us to see that it is powerful even in the lives of believers and that it constantly works to press us into its evil mold.

That raises the question, "In what sense has Christ defeated sin in the believer?" The answer is that he has overthrown its rule, weakened its power, and even killed its root so that it cannot bear the fruit of eternal death in a believer. Still—and this is amazing but true—sin is sin; its nature and purpose remain unchanged; its force and success still grab us by the throat.[4]

2. We find this law inside us. Paul had heard horror stories about sin all his life. He had seen countless bony fingers waving in his face to warn him of sin's power. But in Romans 7:21 he moved from cozy theory into troubling experience: he *found* this law. It is one thing to sit in a group and critique dissertations on original sin; it is something else to find yourself subdued by its strength and madness. It is one thing to listen to a lecture about AIDS—how it spreads, what it does to a body, how invincible it is; it is another thing to hear your doctor say to you, "HIV-positive—I'm sorry."

Few people have come to terms with the law of sin. If more people had, we would hear more complaints of it in prayers, see more struggling against it, and find less of its fruit in the world. When we find this law in us, Paul's "Who shall deliver me?" echoes down our bones.

Believers are the only people who ever find the law of sin at work in them. Unbelievers can't feel it. The law of sin is a raging river, carrying them along; they cannot measure the force of the current, because they have surrendered themselves to it and are borne along by it. A believer, on the other hand, swims upstream—he meets sin head-on and strains under its strength.

3. We find this law when we're at our best. As powerful as this law of sin is, it doesn't rule the heart of the believer. Paul found it at work in him even while *he wanted to do good.* He didn't stumble onto it in a time of great backsliding, or when he was indifferent about the things of God. He was aware of it even when he most wanted to serve God, when he set his mind to obey his Savior and King, when Christ ruled his heart.

Though the law of sin works from the inside and ambushes believers at their best, it isn't their dictator. Believers march to a different Drummer: "I want to do good," Paul says (Romans 7:21)—I want to please God, give him glory, serve his people, honor his name. By God's grace the desire to obey him ordinarily prevails in us, even against this insidious enemy within.[5]

4. This law never rests. Since grace rules the believer's heart, he wants to do good. We can describe that desire in two ways. First, there is his general and constant desire to please God (verse 18). Second, there are times when the believer has a particular duty in mind that he wants to perform, such as private prayer or giving a tenth of his income to God ("When I want to do good"— verse 21). The law of sin opposes both.

The "law of sin and death" is in a constant tug of war against the believer's overall desire to please God (verses 14–25). But sin goes further: when the believer sets his jaw to even the simplest duty to God, sin fights him right at that point ("Evil is right there with me"— verse 21), making him drowsy or distracted when he would pray, or stingy and ambitious when he would tithe.

Don't you sometimes feel like Dr. Jekyll and Mr. Hyde? Every believer who is also a sinner (which is every believer) does. "For the sinful nature desires what is contrary to the Spirit, and the Spirit what is contrary to the sinful nature. They are in conflict with each other, so that you do not do what you want" (Galatians 5:17).

Who shall deliver me?

Wise Up

We are at the beginning of obedience to God. To understand these four truths about indwelling sin is to arm yourself against it. In your struggle against sin, there is only one thing more important to grasp than these four facts: the free, justifying grace of God in Christ's blood. The grace of God in Christ and the law of sin are the two fountains of all your holiness and sin, joy and trouble, refreshment and sorrow. If you are to walk with God and glorify him in this world, you need to master both.

Suppose there is a kingdom that has within its wall two mighty opposing forces. The subjects of the king are at odds, always plotting and feuding against each other. If the king is not wise, his kingdom will be laid in ruins.[6] The law of sin and the law of the Spirit of life (Romans 8:2) in us are mortal enemies. If we are not spiritually wise in managing our souls, how can we help making a wreck of ourselves?

But many people live in darkness and ignorance about their own hearts. They keep careful track of how their investments are doing on Wall Street and get frequent checkups at the doctor; they watch what they eat and work out at the gym three or four times a week to keep their bodies finely tuned. But how many people give the least thought to their souls? If it is important to watch over and care for our bodies and investments, which will soon die and rot, how much more important is it for us to guard our immortal souls?

Getting to know indwelling sin, as humiliating and discouraging as it can be, is our *wisdom*—if we have any interest at all in finding out what pleases the Lord (Ephesians 5:10) and avoiding everything that grieves his Holy Spirit (Ephesians 4:30).

Questions for Reflection and Discussion

1. Read through Romans 7:14–25. Which phrase or phrases best describe your own experience?

2. Can you think of ways the law of sin offers rewards for obeying it and threatens punishment for ignoring it? (This anticipates the next chapter.)

3. Think of a time when you "found" the law of sin in you—when it seemed to take over and bend you to its will even, as it were, against your will. Describe that time to your group, if you can.

4. What do you think is the most frustrating thing about the sin in your heart?

5. If it is true that the law of sin in you never rests, what hope do you have?

6. Read Luke 12:15 and Matthew 26:41. In light of this chapter, describe the daily diligence you need in order to heed Jesus' warnings.

7. What do you hope to gain through studying this book? Write a prayer in the space below, asking God to make it so in your life.

2 | *the long arm of the law*

If a rhinoceros were to enter this restaurant now,
there is no denying he would have great power here.
But I should be the first to rise and assure him
that he had no authority whatever.
—G. K. Chesterton

The Flesh Is a Rhino

The law of sin in believers is like Chesterton's rhino. The
only moral, authoritative rule over believers is the kingdom
and reign of God. Indwelling sin is a usurper to the throne
who, like the rhino, can at times force himself on us. Even
though we rise and tell him he has no authority, he can push
us around the restaurant.

The law of sin pushes us around the same way other laws
motivate our obedience: with promises and threats.
Remember the covenant ceremony acted out in Deuteronomy 27 and 28? Half the tribes of Israel stood on the slope
of Mount Ebal, and the other half across the valley on
Mount Gerizim. Those on Ebal shouted curses on those
who disobey the law; those on Gerizim proclaimed blessings
on the obedient. When there is a power behind such threats

and promises that can make them good, people are motivated to obey.

The Rewards of Sin

The pleasures of sin are the rewards it offers—rewards
most people will sell their souls for. Hebrews 11:24–26 hints
at a battle for the heart of Moses:

> By faith Moses, when he had grown up, refused to be
> known as the son of Pharaoh's daughter. He chose
> to be mistreated along with the people of God rather
> than to enjoy the *pleasures of sin* for a short time. He
> regarded disgrace for the sake of Christ as of greater
> value than the treasures of Egypt, because he was
> looking ahead to his reward.

The contest was between the law of sin and the law of
grace. The rewards offered to Moses by sin must have been
great: honor with the Egyptians, wealth beyond anything he
could see among the people of Israel, the intellectual delights
of debating with the top minds of Egypt, the sensual pleasures
of fine food, women, and entertainment. You can see in your
own heart how compelling and enslaving sin's rewards are.
Moses is one of the few in whom the rewards of *grace* prevailed.

The Punishments of Sin

One thing Moses faced if he didn't bow to sin was a life
of "mistreatment" and "disgrace" (verses 25–26). These are

the threats of punishment for *disobeying* the law of sin (which is to obey God). All sorts of evil, trouble, and danger are promised in this world to those who follow Christ,[1] and sin loves to parade those before believers' eyes.

Besides the suffering for following Christ, there are the hardships of the cross and self-denial that believers are called to, and the hard work of putting sin to death. The writer to the Hebrews even speaks of resisting sin to the point of shedding your blood (Hebrews 12:4). The life of the disciple is not for the timid. Most would rather give in to sin than go through the painful work of picking up a cross and nailing their flesh to it.[2]

An Inside Job

Dante found Brutus, Cassius, and Judas in the deepest pit of hell.[3] Those who are traitors, who win the trust of their friends and then betray from the inside, are the most wicked of all. Indwelling sin is our Judas.

The law of sin doesn't work on us from the outside. We carry it in us. It's not a written law, simply directing us by decree. It is inbred—working, compelling, and urging us from the shadows of our hearts. Paul calls it "sin living in me" (Romans 7:17), the evil that is "right there with me" (verse 21), "another law at work in the members of my body," and "the law of sin at work within my members" (verse 23). In verse 18 he says, "I know that nothing good lives in *me*, that is, in my *sinful nature.*" The law of sin is in some sense *Paul.*

This is why God promises to circumcise his people's

hearts in the old covenant (Deuteronomy 30:6), and to write his law on their hearts in the new (Jeremiah 31:31–33). No mere written law can muster a threat against the law of sin working from the inside. To slap a copy of the Ten Commandments in front of someone under the rule of sin and tell him to submit is as effective as trying to make a rhinoceros jump by whacking him on the rump with a blade of grass. The rhino is oblivious. The glory of the covenant of grace is that in it God's law meets the law of sin on a level playing field, where God's holy law will carry the day.

Sin Gets Under Our Skin

Still, since the law of sin is inside us, it has some irritating advantages:

1. Indwelling sin wears out its welcome. It has settled down in us and is at home (Romans 7:17, 20). If sin only came to visit now and then, like an unwelcome in-law, we could get a lot of godliness done while it was away. If it were like an army that struck, then pulled back for a time, we could refresh ourselves and fortify our defenses during the calm. But the flesh is a relentless homebody and assailant.

Wherever you go, whatever you do, the law of sin is with you step for step—in the best you do, in the worst you do. How often do you think about the fact that you carry around in you a deadly companion?

2. Indwelling sin doesn't observe a sabbath. Just when Paul was ready to do something holy and loving, sin was at his elbow (verse 21). Sin isn't just a permanent houseguest; it's a meddlesome wretch. It's always poking its nose in, looking over your shoulder, whispering in your ear.

Do you want to pray? Listen to a sermon? Meditate on the Word? Give a generous gift to the kingdom? Encourage a brother? Resist temptation? This hateful, wicked pest is in your face with a thousand distractions and surprises, making sure you can't perfectly accomplish the good you intend (verse 18; Galatians 5:17). It exasperates us.

3. Sin does its dirty work with the greatest of ease. Since it works from within, it "easily entangles" us (Hebrews 12:1). It needs no help from the outside (though the world and the Devil are always ready to lend a hand). There is no spiritual duty, nothing godly you can set yourself to, in which you won't feel the wind of sin's resistance in your face. Does God command you to believe he is good and wise when you lose a friend? Indwelling sin sidles up with seeds of doubt and mistrust. Does God command you to help a neighbor in need? There is sin with apathy and stinginess in hand. Does God want you to long for the coming of Christ? Here is sin, dangling before your eyes the trinkets of the world.

Are You Wrestling the Rhino?

If you've read this chapter and seen a rough horn lowered at your soul, your own flesh snorting and pawing and ready to charge, there's hope. The more you discover the power of indwelling sin, the less you will suffer its effects. Because the better you know this rhino, the more you will hate it; and to the length that you abhor it—and no far-ther—you will grasp for grace against it.

But if you don't find yourself dodging the rhino's horn day and night in a struggle against sin, it may be that you've made peace with the rhino. You are willingly, happily under its power and rule. In that case, you should doubt that you are born of God. No one who is born of God can live at peace with sin (1 John 3:9). I appeal to you, for the sake of your soul: Run to Christ! Only he can slay the rhino in your heart.

Questions for Reflection and Discussion

1. If the claims of this chapter are true, then what obligations are believers under to know the power of indwelling sin? How can knowing the power of the flesh help us?

2. On the other hand, if these claims are true, what danger might there be for us if we ignore indwelling sin? How is it possible to ignore this rhino?

3. What weapons do you think you need in order to combat this enemy within you? How can you bring them to bear against indwelling sin?

4. Make a list of the rewards offered by the law of sin for adultery, vengeance, gossip, and spiritual lazi-ness. Which rewards do you find most enticing?

5. Make a list of some of the burdens and crosses demanded by Christ's call to follow him at work or school, in marriage or ministry. Which burdens do you least want to carry? Which crosses are you most reluctant to shoulder?

3 | *the haunted house*

Poor intricated soul! Riddling,
perplexed, labyrinthical soul!
—John Donne

"I'll go in if you will."

"Maybe we should go home—it's late—I didn't tell my parents."

"Chicken!"

"Am not!—it's just—we don't have time."

"Oh, you're scared all right—you believe the stories, don't you?"

"Okay, Mr. 'No Fear,' we'll go in—but if I get grounded, you'll pay."

"It's a deal. Let's go."

The boy and girl push through a wrought-iron gate that hangs by one hinge and enter an unkempt court-yard. Dead leaves scurry across a walk, and a decayed Victorian mansion in front of them groans against a sudden wind. The sky mourns overhead, and thunderbolts dance above the gables.

So begins every haunted-house scene in every horror movie ever made. After one of the heroes puts his foot through a rotted plank of the porch, they find the door unlocked and step inside, while we whisper, "Don't do it!" We follow them through cobweb-littered halls and rooms, our pulse quick and breath short, knowing some horrid thing will jump, fall, or fly out of a closet, through a window, from behind a door—or maybe it will grab one of them in the basement or attic. Or, better, under the stairs they'll find a secret passageway that leads to what looks to be an abandoned laboratory. On a slab there is a cloth covering a body. Fools that they are, our heroes pull back the cover—a disfigured face makes them jump, but it is still, eyes closed. They turn to go, and we relax. Then the creature rises and nabs them from behind!

The haunted house scares us because it hides something unknown and deadly. It has countless coat closets, cabinets, false walls, trapdoors, attics, basements—corners and shadows where the monster lies in wait, licking its chops.

You have a haunted house within you: your heart.

The Haunted Heart

The heart is a maze that only God can solve (Jeremiah 17:9–10). Computers can't decipher its floor plan. We modestly admit we don't know someone else's heart, but the truth is we can't even know our own. Do you always know why you choose chocolate over vanilla? Why one day your passions sizzle and another you're a dead leaf in the wind? Can you number all the events and images that impress your heart and make it lean this way or that? Haven't you been surprised by the insincerity and even intrigue you've found in your heart?

But the heart is more than complicated and unsearchable: it is "deceitful above all things" (verse 9). Every night Tom Brokaw tells us about shady politics and business scams. People finding loopholes in the law to use their sweat-earned money to build stately pleasure domes in Xanadu. But the sleaziest back-room Mafia deal can't equal the deceitfulness in your heart. The heart is "deceitful above *all* things."

Do you doubt it? Think how fickle you are. One day you're a sage, the next a clown. You can be open and cheery or reserved and gloomy, easy to get along with or a real crank, romantic or frosty. One day Jesus is all the world to you; the next, you love the world more than King Midas did.

And think of your inconsistencies. Your mind says tithing is right, and your will puts the money in the plate— but all the while you wish God weren't so demanding. Or you know that secret communion with God is a feast for your soul, and you long for it—but you can't roll out of bed, or if you do, your mind zooms everywhere in the universe except to heaven. Or your mind knows that lust is evil and dangerous, but you put yourself to sleep at night imagining a weekend in Monterey with the hunk two apartments down.

The Hidden Horrors

This unsearchable, deceitful heart is where sin hides. The Preacher said, "The hearts of men, moreover, are full of evil and there is madness in their hearts while they live"

(Ecclesiastes 9:3). Jesus called the heart the fountain of sin (Matthew 15:19), and a treasure chest where we sock away evil (Luke 6:45). Put all this together and you have a scene no director could stage. He could never design a house as complex as your heart, or gather enough monsters to fill it.

What Is This Heart?

Heart is used different ways in the Bible. Sometimes it is the mind believing or being enlightened (Romans 10:10; Ephesians 1:18), the will deciding and acting (2 Corinthians 9:7; Ephesians 6:6), or the affections[1] feeling (2 Corinthians 2:4). In Hebrews 4:12 the heart thinks *and* feels. The best way to think of your heart is that it comprises

- your thoughts, plans, judgments, discernment (the *mind*);
- your choices and actions (the *will*);
- your longings, desire, revulsion, imagination, feelings (the *affections*);
- your sense of right and wrong, which approves or condemns your mind, will, and affections (the *conscience*).

All this is unsearchable and deceitful above all things.

But the believer has a *new* heart (Ezekiel 36:26), a *new* mind—even the mind of *Christ* (Romans 7:25; 8:26; 1 Corinthians 2:16), and new *desires* for the things of God (Romans 7:18; 2 Corinthians 5:2; Hebrews 13:18). Yet, God's work in this renewed heart is unfinished (1 John 3:2). The mind can't see as clearly as it will (1 Corinthians 13:9, 12), the desires can be entangled (Galatians 2:11–13), and the will can't fully do God's will (Galatians 5:17). The flesh in the believer remains unsearchable and deceitful.

Advantage, Flesh

How would you like to fight an enemy who, just when you had him on the ropes, could duck into a cave or tunnel where you couldn't follow? An enemy who could hide just out of reach, letting you rest long enough to think he was gone for good, then drop from nowhere onto your back? This is the advantage of indwelling sin—it lurks in an unsearchable and deceitful fortress, where you can't find him.

Have you ever battled some lust—prayed and fasted and sought counsel against it—then watched it slink away into the night? You thought you had it licked. You thought you could move on in your spiritual life. But one day you were watching television, and a commercial for Calvin Klein jeans bubbled up a whole nest of wicked desires. Sin can be like trick birthday candles: you blow them out and smile, thinking you have your wish; then your jaw drops as they burst into flames.

No Surrender

Never think for a minute that the war against sin is over in this life. There isn't even a cease-fire. Many generals have been surprised because they were careless after a victory.

Countless believers have been ambushed on the heels of a giant step forward in faith. David, for example, lived a long life of devotion and duty to God, and saw mercy on mercy from God's hands; then sin tip-toed up behind him in the dark and stabbed him in the back.

If you violently war against your flesh, you'll win ground. It will grow weak, and you'll grow in grace into the image of Christ. Still, the work has to be endless as long as we're in this world. If you cut the flesh any slack, you'll watch it regroup and revive. You may even end up worse off than you were before (compare Luke 11:24–26).

Heed the warnings that fill the Scriptures:

> Therefore, since we are surrounded by such a great cloud of witnesses, let us throw off everything that hinders and the sin that so easily entangles, and let us run with perseverance the race marked out for us. Let us fix our eyes on Jesus, the author and perfecter of our faith, who for the joy set before him endured the cross, scorning its shame, and sat down at the right hand of the throne of God. Consider him who endured such opposition from sinful men, so that you will not grow weary and lose heart.
>
> In your struggle against sin, you have not yet resisted to the point of shedding your blood. (Hebrews 12:1–4)

> "Be careful," Jesus said to them. "Be on your guard against the yeast of the Pharisees and Sadducees." (Matthew 16:6)

"Watch and pray so that you will not fall into temptation. The spirit is willing, but the body is weak." (Matthew 26:41)

Then [Jesus] said to them, "Watch out! Be on your guard against all kinds of greed; a man's life does not consist in the abundance of his possessions." (Luke 12:15)

Be on your guard; stand firm in the faith; be men of courage; be strong. (1 Corinthians 16:13)

Therefore, dear friends, since you already know this, be on your guard so that you may not be carried away by the error of lawless men and fall from your secure position. (2 Peter 3:17)

Advantage, Believer

As endless and complicated as this war is, believers rush in with confidence: the Holy Spirit takes the horror out of the horror show. We don't know our hearts, but he does (Psalm 139). He is a blazing torch we carry into the haunted house, and he ferrets out the monsters. He leads us into a closet under the stairs and uncovers a seething hatred. He shines under the bed and exposes a sniveling lust. No sin escapes his searching eye.

> Search me, O God, and know my heart;
> test me and know my anxious thoughts.

See if there is any offensive way in me,
and lead me in the way everlasting.
(verses 23–24)

Questions for Reflection and Discussion

1. Many Christians are convinced that the flesh can be beaten in a single crisis event so that they can move on to a life free of struggle with sin. What do you think?[2]

2. If you agree that the battle against the flesh never ends in this life, why do you think God has set things up that way? Why do you think we would prefer a one-time-knock-down-drag-out fight to settle it?

3. Under the heading "No Surrender," there is a list of many warnings from Scripture. Describe specific ways you can heed those warnings.

4. The Spirit is our only sure help to search out the sins hiding in our hearts. Using Psalm 139 as your starting point, take one day each for your mind, will, and affections. Meditate on the work of the Spirit. Then ask him to search your heart, and dredge up the worst sins he can find. Confess them, weep over them, and hate them. Ask Christ's mercy and the Spirit's help to crush them.

4 | *irreconcilable differences*

Towards thee I roll, thou all-destroying but
unconquering whale; to the last I grapple with thee;
from hell's heart I stab at thee; for hate's sake
I spit my last breath at thee.
—Herman Melville

Flawless Hatred

Literature smolders with hatred: Shylock aches for his pound of flesh in *The Merchant of Venice.* Javert dogs Jean Valjean through sixteen hundred pages of *Les Miserables.* C. S. Lewis's arch-villain Weston degenerates from thug in *Out of the Silent Planet* to "un-man" in *Perelandra,* ripping open the backs of frogs with his thumbnail and leaving them to die. But none of these can sustain a pure hatred to match Captain Ahab's eternal malice in *Moby Dick.* Ahab chases the White Whale across the oceans of the world. He doesn't blink to forfeit his ship and every life it carries, if only he can heave his harpoon into that terrible eye.

Moby Dick is a picture of our savage battle: let the White Whale stand for God—but don't be quick to make Captain Ahab the flesh. Ahab is the whale's *enemy,* but Paul says the flesh is more than God's enemy: it is the *enmity*, the hostility, the pure hatred itself.

> The carnal mind is enmity against God; for it is not subject to the law of God, nor indeed can be.[1] (Romans 8:7 NKJV)

If the whale is God and Ahab's *hatred* is the flesh, then who is Captain Ahab?

You were.

Impossible Peace

Two enemies, no matter how deep the river of their bitterness runs, can make peace—but only if the hostility between them is destroyed. It is impossible to make peace with hostility itself. So when Paul identifies the flesh with enmity and hatred of God, he cuts off any hope that the flesh will bow to God or befriend him. A treaty between God and the flesh is impossible.

In Romans 5:10 Paul says we were God's enemies—we were all of us Captain Ahabs. Christ is the peacemaker in the gospel, using his death to put to death the hostility between us and God.[2] Our "old man" (the flesh) was crucified with Christ (Romans 6:6), rendering it powerless to rule over us and enslave us and bear the fruit of eternal death in us. When he appears, he will annihilate the flesh forever. This is the only way to deal with enmity: destroy it.

But every drop of poison is poison; every spark of fire is fire; and the last bit of flesh that remains in the believer is still enmity. When God's grace changes our nature, it doesn't change the nature of the flesh. It conquers it, weakens it, mortally wounds it, so that we are no longer Captain Ahabs by nature; yet his defiant malice smolders in our flesh. By the time Paul wrote Romans, he must have been as Christlike as anyone can expect to be this side of heaven, and he surely spent his days putting his flesh to death. Still he cried out for deliverance from this irreconcilable enemy.

> What a wretched man I am! Who will deliver me from this body of death? (Romans 7:24)

Groaning for Heaven

God is love. His nature is unmixed beauty and loveliness. He is eternally excellent, and infinitely to be desired above any creature. He has showered his beauty and love on us in his Son, making us new people in him, filling us with hope and expectations of one day living with him in his home, the throne room of love. But the remains of the flesh leave us in an anxious position. Against this God we carry in us an enmity that cannot be appeased.

This is the wearying power of sin in the believer: it won't accept a cease-fire, much less a peace treaty. So how can we expect to have any rest from the flesh except by putting it to death? How can we hope for complete freedom from it except in heaven?

An invading army can sometimes be persuaded to put down its guns by being given what it wants: a piece of land, or a promise of tribute. Some people think they can quiet the flesh's rage the same way. So they look for ways to "gratify the desires of the flesh" (Romans 13:14). This is to put out fire with gasoline. Sin won't quench the flesh, only stoke it.

Enemy Enough

You won't get to be the heavyweight champion of the world by going fifteen rounds with Woody Allen. To be the greatest, you have to knock off the reigning champ. The flesh has chosen quite an enemy: it is "enmity against *God.*" Sometimes we think of the flesh as *our* enemy; but it only hates us because God is in us: "The flesh wars against the Spirit" in us (Galatians 5:17).

Which is easier: to sit with a bucket of butter-soaked popcorn and watch Tom Cruise on the big screen for two hours, or kneel and pray for five minutes? Tom Cruise wins hands down, because there is literally no competition. What the flesh hates is God, so it resists anything that smacks of God—especially communion with him. The flesh can curl up by your side and watch mindless movies all night long. But let even the barest thought of meditations flutter into your mind, and the flesh goes to Red Alert. Before you get past "Our Father," your eyes, which were glued to the screen, now sag in sleepiness, and your attention, which was so fixed on the plot, now zips around the universe faster than the Starship Enterprise.

The flesh's hatred of God explains a lot. Think about worship. In its essence, worship is high communion with God, and so the flesh should cringe at the door of the sanctuary. But what if a person wants to perform the outward forms of worship without approaching God in his heart? He may want to do his duty in worship, like a Pharisee looking for brownie points with God. Or he may like the music at church because it rocks. Or maybe just being in a church building makes him feel secure. Will the flesh lift a finger to excommunicate that kind of worshiper?

You can feel the hostility of the flesh whenever you approach God—it makes real love for him into work: Digging around the Bible to find a juicy new insight to impress your small group is like sailing the Caribbean, but poring over the Scriptures to find the Lover of your soul is like skiing *up* Mount Everest. Conjuring up a happy mood with some music you don't even know the words to is like solving 2 + 2 with a calculator. But savoring the glory of Christ and his tender love until your heart is softened toward him is like using mental math to calculate pi to the thousandth place. And giving a birthday present to your best friend is like forcing down some double-fudge brownies. But giving up your extra bedroom to a homeless person in the name of Jesus is like eating the Rockies for breakfast.[3]

I Hate Everything About You

A husband and wife on the verge of divorce have hope if they can just find a spot of common ground. If they both like ice fishing, for example, a weekend on a frozen lake can be a calm place in their domestic storm. They might even rediscover their team spirit while landing a 56-inch northern pike.

If there were the least thing about God that the flesh could appreciate, the believer could have a constant shelter and retreat from sin and its hatred. If the flesh didn't mind God's wisdom, for example, the soul could meditate on the mystery of the gospel day and night without tiring, and find constant strength in God's plan to save him. But the flesh hates everything about God. Since it resists everything about God, it resists every way we try to taste him and know him and love him. And the more something enables us to find God and feast on him, the more violently the flesh fights against it.

It takes its battle to every quarter of the soul: When the mind wants to know God, the flesh imposes ignorance, darkness, error, and trivial thoughts. The will can't move toward God without feeling the weight of stubbornness holding it back. And the affections, longing to long for God, are constantly fighting the infection of sensuality or the disease of indifference.

Our Captain's Curse

Captain Ahab was driven by his rage to chase the whale to the end. The flesh is just as driven, and will with its last breath spit at God. But there is in us a Warrior just as committed to the flesh's destruction. The Spirit wars against the flesh (Galatians 5:17). Filled with the Spirit, empowered by God's love of us and our love for him, we turn on the flesh with our Captain's own curse:

> Towards thee I roll, thou all-destroying but unconquering flesh; to the last I grapple with thee; from heaven's heart I stab at thee; for love's sake I spit my last breath at thee.

Questions for Reflection and Discussion

1. Can you explain, using concepts from this chapter, why Israel so easily turned from the true worship of God to bowing down to idols, and even sacrificing their children to Moloch? Does this also help explain why modern false religions and cults often seem to prosper and grow more easily than the one true religion?

2. What do you think about someone who says he doesn't find this hatred seething somewhere inside him?

3. How does this chapter make you feel toward your flesh?

4. What are some ways you have tried to make peace with your flesh, or appease it? Describe the results. What happens when a person tries to get relief from the flesh by gratifying it (for example, trying to make lust go away by giving in to illicit sexual desires)?

5. Spend time thinking about what you will be like when your flesh is finally disintegrated. How will you be freer to love God? Try to imagine your love specifically as *your* love at last liberated, rather than as generic love.

part two

The Power of Sin in How It Works

Trust me.
—Herman Melville
The Confidence Man

5 | *the tricks of the trade*

deceive /dɪ' siv/ v. ME. [(O)Fr. deceivre, deçoivre
f. L decipere, f. de- DE- I + capere take, seize;
or f. deceiv- tonic stem of deceveir (mod. décevoir)
f. Proto-Romance alt. of L decipere.] † 1 v.t. Trap or overcome
by trickery; take unawares by craft or guile; lead astray. ME-L18
2 v.t. Cause to believe what is false; delude, take in. . . .
—The New Shorter Oxford English Dictionary

The Traveling Salvation Show

Huck Finn meets two grifters, the self-styled Duke of Bridgewater and the Dauphin himself, "Looy the Seventeen, son of Looy the Sixteen and Marry Antonette." In one of their cons, the "Dauphin" takes Huck to a camp meeting, where they watch the preacher whip the crowd into a Pentecostal frenzy of *hallelujahs* and tears at the mourning bench. The Dauphin gets "agoing" himself, louder than the whole crowd of a thousand. The preacher calls him up to the platform to tell his story. Huck relates it to us:

> He told them he was a pirate—been a pirate for thirty years, out in the Indian Ocean, and his crew

was thinned out considerable, last spring, in a fight, and he was home now, to take out some fresh men, and thanks to goodness he'd been robbed last night, and put ashore off of a steamboat without a cent, and he was glad of it, it was the blessedest thing that ever happened to him, because he was a changed man now, and happy for the first time in his life; and poor as he was, he was going to start right off and work his way back to the Indian Ocean and put in the rest of his life trying to turn the pirates into the true path; for he could do it better than anybody else, being acquainted with all the pirate crews in that ocean; and though it would take him a long time to get there, without money, he would get there anyway, and every time he convinced a pirate he would say to him, "Don't you thank me, don't you give me no credit, it all belongs to them dear people in Pokeville camp-meeting, natural brothers and benefactors of the race—and that dear preacher there, the truest friend a pirate ever had!"[1]

When the pirate-Dauphin bursts into tears, the crowd calls for a collection. They even ask him to pass his own hat around. He humbly obliges, with many sobbing words of blessing on the kind people of Pokeville. They invite him to stay for a week, but the good-hearted pirate respectfully declines their hospitality. "He was in a sweat to get to the Indian Ocean right off and go to work on the pirates."[2]

This is the art of deception: *to make someone believe that things are other than they are, so that he will do something he would never otherwise do.* This is the way your flesh makes you into the willing servant of sin.

In the Beginning Was the Con

As long as Eve could see things clearly, she was fine. But when the Serpent deceived her, she ate (Genesis 3:13). When Adam followed her, sin entered the world. Trickery always has been and always will be Satan's *modus operandi.* No one would follow him if he or she weren't taken in (Revelation 12:9; 20:10).

The apple didn't fall far from the tree. The law of sin in us, since it springs from its father the Devil, works the same way: "But encourage one another daily, as long as it is called Today, so that none of you may be hardened by sin's *deceitfulness*" (Hebrews 3:13). Paul says that before Christ freed us, we were "foolish, disobedient, *deceived* and enslaved by all kinds of passions and pleasures" (Titus 3:3). He tells us to put off our old self (the flesh, the law of sin in us), because it is "being corrupted by its *deceitful* desires" (Ephesians 4:22). And over and over when God warns us against sin, he cautions us to watch out for its treachery.[3] In fact, you can write this down as a maxim: When the flesh deceives you, you *will* sin.

The Flesh Blows Your Mind

If you want to overthrow a fortress, start by knocking out the watchman—if he can't warn the others, you will easily breach the wall and carry the day. The flesh plies deceit to knock out the watchman of your soul: your *mind.*

Each of the faculties of your soul has duties before God. The *mind* is the sentinel, commanded to watch carefully over the soul by questioning, assessing, and making judgments: "Will this please God?" "Is this according to God's Word?" If the mind determines that an action is right, the *affections* should then fall in line and desire, long for, and cling to that which the mind said was good. Last, the *will* puts the soul into action, carrying out what the mind said was good and the affections hungered for. When each does its job, you obey God from the heart.[4]

You can see what a mess deception makes of obedience. If your mind is persuaded to believe a sin is good for your soul, and your affections work up an appetite for it, your will gives its consent—the dominoes fall and the flesh bears its putrid fruit in your life.[5]

The Master of Disguise

Deception is a fact of life. We shake our heads when *20/20* uncovers another con man who dupes the elderly out of their life savings by selling them investment property in the middle of the Okefenokee Swamp, or pounding two thousand nails into a stud in the attic and charging a dollar a nail for "repairs" to the roof. At times we cheer deception, as when the winsome scoundrels Johnny Hooker (Robert Redford) and Henry Gondorff (Paul Newman) stick it to the loathsome Doyle Lonnegan (Robert Shaw) in *The Sting*. But deception isn't just swirling around outside us; it's a fact of life inside us, working the same way any grifter on the midway robs you blind: by concealing, hiding, and disguising the truth.

The deceiver disguises what is undesirable and harmful (the hook in the fishing lure, for example) beneath what he thinks we want (a brightly colored fly, if you're a fish). He hides from our minds the painful consequences we ought to consider (if you bite the hook, you'll be captured, cleaned, and cooked), so that we make a false judgment. He is subtle, alluring, patient when he needs to be, pushy when he has to be, and he knows our weaknesses. He has one goal in mind and is unscrupulous in his pursuit of it.

The Anatomy of Sin's Seduction

To understand how the flesh dupes us, consider James 1:14–15 in light of the principles of deception:

> . . . each one is tempted when, by his own evil desire, he is dragged away and enticed. Then, after desire has conceived, it gives birth to sin; and sin, when it is full-grown, gives birth to death.

James is writing to people trying to excuse their sin much the way Adam and Eve did in the Garden, pinning the blame on God. But James says that the whole guilt of sin lies in the sinner, as he is hoodwinked by the desires of his own flesh. He helps us unmask the con man within by exposing what the flesh wants, and how it goes about getting it from us.

First, the goal the flesh aims at is *death* (verse 15). Whatever sin pretends, it will end in death.[6] The flesh wants us to believe that the consequences for dallying with sin will only be slight (not as much blessing from God, a cheaper seat in heaven). Knowing this is our first means of arming ourselves against deceit (as knowing that the used-car salesman will do anything to sell you a car helps to protect you from driving home the lemon while he laughs behind your back).[7]

Second, the way the flesh works for your death is by *temptation* (verse 14). The essence of temptation is deceit—to be tempted and to be deceived are the same thing. And James lists what we can call five degrees of temptation:

(1)   dragging away (the *mind*),
(2)   enticing (the *affections*),
(3)   conceiving sin (in the *will*),
(4)   the birth of sin (in actions, words, thoughts, and so on),
(5)   death by sin. (Enslavement to sin is spiritual death.)

The first degree relates to the mind—it is dragged away from its duties by the deceit of sin. The second aims at the affections—they are enticed and entangled. The third overcomes the will—the consent of the will is the conception of actual sin. The fourth degree disrupts our way of life as sin is born into it. The fifth is the flesh's goal, a hardened life of sin, which leads to eternal death.

This fifth degree, by God's grace, is never reached in true believers. God also often aborts conceived sin[8] in the believer's life (the fourth degree), sparing us many burdens. But one means he uses to prevent our falling into sin is to warn us of the first three degrees. So we will meticulously lay them open to the light. In chapters 6 and 7 we'll expose the flesh's mind games. In chapter 8 we'll see how it entangles the affections. In chapter 9 we'll consider the actual consent to sin and how the flesh wheedles the will into it.

Our hope is to see the con man within us exposed and come to the same end as the Duke and the Dauphin in *Huckleberry Finn:* tarred and feathered and run out of town on a rail.

Questions for Reflection and Discussion

1. Think of the best magic trick you've ever seen. What made it work on you?

2. Have you ever been really taken by a salesman? How did he hook you? What strategy did he use, and why was it effective? Has your flesh ever worked you over the same way to get you into a sin? Tell what happened.

3. We saw that the Serpent's deception in the garden became the same pattern used by the flesh in our lives. Look closely at the story of the Fall, in Genesis 3:1–6. How did the Serpent persuade Eve to eat? Describe his deception in detail: What did he hide or disguise? What did he accentuate, and how did he make sin attractive?

4. Without looking ahead to the next two chapters, make a list of what you think some of the duties of the mind are in obeying God. (Remember the image of the mind as the watchman of the soul). For each you think of, describe how you think the flesh drags your mind away from those duties.

6 | *getting carried away*

It is wonderful, when a calculation is made,
how little the mind is actually employed
in the discharge of any profession.
—Samuel Johnson

Dinner with the Boss's Wife

For the past seven years you've been the top salesman at
Southwest International Napkin Supply (SINS). Your boss has
offered you a partnership in SINS, and asked you to dinner at
his home to discuss the details of your promotion. As you turn
into his cobblestone drive and get cleared through the front
gate, your mind swirls with schemes of the grand villa you'll
soon be able to build yourself. You're living your dream.

The servant greets you at the door, and shows you to the
dining room. There the boss's wife, apparently dressed for a
private evening with her husband, greets you with a warmer-
than-usual kiss on the cheek and dismisses her servant for
the evening. She hooks her right arm inside your left, and
walks you toward the dining table, which you notice is set for
only two. "Bolero" is playing in the background, and two tall
white candles burn in settings of silver.

"Where's Dan?" you ask, not catching on.

"Oh—didn't you get the message?" she asks, as if there really were one. "He had to fly to Buenos Aires to meet with a supplier who's threatening to raise prices. It'll just be the two of us for the *whole* evening. I'm really looking forward to going over our new partnership in SINS."

Beads of perspiration begin to tickle your forehead. Your mind races to size up the situation: you've always thought Carolyn a handsome woman, and wearing that gown, and in this setting, she's downright striking. All the servants have left the grounds—the mansion is deserted, but for the two of you. Dan won't be back till next week, and your wife is visiting her mother in Lincoln. From the way Carolyn is leaning against you, her nose almost touching your collar so that you can feel her warm breath, you know exactly what she expects of you. If you give it to her, she'll likely hurry you up the corporate ladder, just as you've always wanted. But if you walk away—if you offend this Empress—you can kiss your new Jag good-bye.

What's it going to be?

The Castle Wall

One man in history passed this test with flying colors: Joseph. The answer he gave to his boss's wife teaches us a double duty of the mind that is our first line of defense against the flesh's deceptions:

> Now Joseph was well-built and handsome, and after a while his master's wife took notice of Joseph and said, "Come to bed with me!"

But he refused. "With me in charge," he told her, "my master does not concern himself with anything in the house; everything he owns he has entrusted to my care. No one is greater in this house than I am. My master has withheld nothing from me except you, because you are his wife. How then could I do such a wicked thing and sin against God?" And though she spoke to Joseph day after day, he refused to go to bed with her or even be with her. (Genesis 39:6–10)

Joseph's mind was protected by two thoughts: the vileness of sin ("How then could I do such a *wicked* thing?") and God's grace and goodness ("How then could I . . . sin *against God?*"). Because his mind was prepared for action (1 Peter 1:13–16), he could see through the deceit of the flesh and resist temptation—though it was overwhelmingly powerful and to resist would cost him more than most men could bear. He risked his life rather than sin.[1]

Remember that the mind is the watchman of the soul, commanded to judge and determine whether something is good and pleasing to God, so the affections can long for it and the will can choose it. If the mind fails to identify a sin as evil, wicked, vile, and bitter, the affections will not be safe from clinging to it, nor the will from giving consent. This is one side of the castle wall, the first line of defense: to keep in mind that every sin is a forsaking of God (Jeremiah 2:19), to never forget the polluting, corrupting, defiling power of sin—to be shaken to the core by how much God loathes sin.[2]

When Paul said Christ's love compelled him (2 Corinthians 5:14), he described the other side of this first defense: the mind must stay fixed on God, especially on his grace and goodness toward us. His love propels, fuels, drives us to obey. It is the fountain of our obedience, and our highest motive to finding out what pleases the Lord[3] and doing it.

In order to walk before God, this is the mind's first duty: to know and hold on to the evil of sin and the love of God. This is how Joseph stood up against overwhelming temptation.

The Breach in the Wall

By now you may have guessed that the law of sin in us, as much as it hates God and as deceitful as it is, doesn't throw up its arms in surrender at this first line of defense. The flesh has its explosives ready to undermine the wall. Its first and most wretched attack is to abuse God's grace in order to make sin seem less sinful, less dangerous, less threatening.

You must understand this: the flesh weakens conviction against sin by separating the *remedy* of grace from the *design* of grace. The Scriptures teach nothing more clearly than that God's design in showing mercy is to make us holy people: "For the grace of God that brings salvation has appeared to all men. It teaches us to say 'No' to ungodliness and worldly passions, and to live self-controlled, upright and godly lives in this present age" (Titus 2:11–12). But God also provides a remedy for our lapses: his loving pardon gives us peace, so that we know that if we do sin, "we have one who speaks to the Father in our defense" (1 John 2:1).

The flesh works to make you forget the design (that you are saved to be holy) and think only of the remedy (if you sin you'll be forgiven). It preaches half a gospel (a twisted gospel) to us: "Go ahead and indulge—it's already paid for." Those who fall prey to such deception are evidently many, since the Scriptures go to such lengths to condemn it (Romans 3:5–8; 6:1–4; Jude 4).

You know the flesh has made a breach in your defenses when your heart is hardened by its deceitfulness (Hebrews 3:13) so that you are careless about sin. You will look at your life and think about how often you need God's forgiveness, and so think of it as something common, nothing to worry over or take pains about. You'll know you are hardened when you begin to extend the boundaries of Christian freedom to include indulgences that in the past would have shocked you. Your flesh will whisper to you that strictness and anxious care about obedience are *legalism*—the gospel came to deliver you from such things! And besides, if you really do commit a sin, you can be forgiven later.

Besides belittling sin, the flesh uses its wiles to drive every thought of God from our minds by filling the mind with thoughts of the world. The flesh knows a mind cannot be fixed on both God and earthly things (Colossians 3:2; 1 John 2:15). The main ploy of the flesh is to slip worldliness into the mind under the guise of *necessity*.

Look at the story of the wedding banquet in Matthew 22. When the feast is ready, the king sends his servants to gather the guests. But each one has an excuse, something more pressing: "They paid no attention and went off—one to his field, another to his business" (verse 5). Working your field can be pleasing to God—he wants us to work hard. You can run a business to God's glory and even use it to extend his kingdom. But the flesh is doing something subtle here—taking what can be good and pleasing to God and using it to squeeze out thoughts of God.

It isn't hard to imagine a man starting off in his business with his heart set on honoring God in all his ways, then being led astray. He gives a tenth or more of his profits to the kingdom, and God blesses his work. So he works harder, makes more profit, gives more to God. This looks and feels like God's blessing, yet his hard work and the demands of his success start to encroach on his time in the Word and private prayer. He meditates more now on his quality control than God's control of his life. The tunnel has been dug under the wall, and it caves in, exposing his heart to the deeper deceit of the flesh.

The Cross-Eyed Watchman

Your mind can only protect against the deceit of the flesh if you are cross-eyed. That is, you can only keep the rottenness of sin and the kindness of God in mind if you fix your eyes on the *cross*. What shows God's hatred of sin more than the cross? What shows God's love to you more than the cross? If you want to know exactly what sin deserves, you have to understand the cross. If you want to know how infinitely deep the rot of sin reaches, you have to think through all the implications of the cross. If you want to know how far God was willing to go to rescue you from sin, you have to see his precious Son hanging on the cross for *you*.

Then, even if it costs you your job and your dreams, you can tell Carolyn to take her candle-lit dinner for two and jump in the lake—or, better, to save it for her husband.

Questions for Reflection and Discussion

1. Look over the story of Joseph and Potiphar's wife in Genesis 39. Make a list of the rewards that sin offered Joseph. Now make a list of the punishments of sin that he had to consider. Have you ever been confronted by a temptation that had so much in its favor? Describe the situation.

2. Is there anything you can think of that makes sin truly *revolting* to you, so that you are repulsed by the thought of it? What is it?

3. Is there anything you can think of that makes God's love seem more real than your best friend's smile? What is it?

4. Brainstorm ways that the flesh distracts you from thinking about sin as revolting and God's love as real.

5. Take some time to examine your heart to find places you might have listened to the flesh's half-gospel. Ask the Holy Spirit to help you (Psalm 139:23–24). Ask him whether there are "Christian freedoms" you are taking that you would have condemned in the past. If there are, ask God to show you whether this is true liberty or you've listened to the flesh.

6. Start your prayers every morning this week by fixing your eyes on the cross. Each day think about a dif-

ferent aspect of the cross that shows the shame of sin, and a different aspect that sheds light on the love of God. At the end of the week, describe any effects this has on your prayers or your ability to resist temptation.

7 | *no idle mind*

John Henry was a li'l baby, uh-huh,
Sittin' on his mama's knee, oh, yeah,
Said: "De Big Bend Tunnel on de C. & O. road
Gonna cause de death of me,
Lawd, Lawd, gonna cause de death of me."

John Henry's Hammer

John Henry was a man. He out-dug the steam drill through the mountain, fifteen feet to nine. He drove so hard he broke his poor heart,

An' he lied down his hammer an' he died,
Lawd, Lawd, he lied down his hammer an' he died.

When we sing the legend of John Henry to our children, we sing the song of a hero. We sing up a storm of celebration as the sweat flies like rain off of John Henry's body, and the wind from his swinging hammer roars through the tunnel. We exalt his hard work, his determination, his skill, his heart. He held nothing back—he gave his life to the work.

John Henry had a hammer. John Henry had a strong arm. Would the mountain have given way to the hammer without his arm? Or to his arm without the hammer?

We stand before the flesh like John Henry before the virgin mountain. We have a Himalayan job before us, and our lives are on the line.

> For if you live according to the [flesh], you will die;
> but if by the Spirit you put to death the misdeeds of
> the body, you will live. (Romans 8:13)

The job is to kill the flesh. The strength we have is the Spirit in us. And God has given us tools to finish the job. Yet to the flesh's delight, most Christians are ignorant of the power of these tools and how to use them. Some attack the mountain with their bare hands and die in their folly. Others sit in the shadow of the mountain polishing their tools till the rocks fall on them and crush them. Believers who take up God's hammer and crush the flesh are as rare as John Henry.

God's Hammer

We said in the last chapter that the flesh works by deceit and that its primary target is the believer's mind. We also said that the believer, to protect himself against deceit, has to fix in his mind the sinfulness of sin and the grace of God. The tools God has given you enable you to do that—when you swing God's hammer, the law of sin is flattened before you.

On the other hand, precisely because these tools are so destructive, the flesh opposes them with all its wily strength. So we have to know not only how to use them, but how to keep from being tricked out of using them.

These great tools of the mind are *meditation* and *private prayer*.

"Now wait a minute," you may protest. "I thought you said most believers are ignorant of these super-tools. But I read my Bible almost every day, and I'm always praying for my kids to be safe and for my neighbor to be a Christian. If *that's* all it takes to lick the flesh, I've pretty near done him in!"

Of course, reading your Bible and praying for others are spiritual duties, and when done in faith and dependence on the Spirit, they will weaken the flesh. But Bible reading is not meditation, and intercession, though crucial, is not the prayer I intend.

The meditation and prayer I mean are designed specifically to ruin the flesh. In this meditation and prayer we compare our hearts to the Scriptures, comparing our lives to what we find there. We ponder the truth as it is in Jesus, to see his life formed in us. But we never approach meditation and prayer like this until we keep three things in mind:

1. Meditate on God with God. Fill your mind with thoughts of God's character, glory, majesty, love, beauty, and goodness—but not abstractly and impersonally, as you might contemplate a textbook description of photosynthesis. Speak *to* God as you contemplate him, humbling your soul before him, adoring and admiring him, delighting in him and giving him glory. Make your meditation into the worship of the psalmist:

> O LORD, my Lord, how majestic is your name in all the earth![1] (Psalm 8:1)

2. Meditate on the Word in the Word. Study the written Word to know the living Word. Never let it be your goal to search the Scriptures to find a new insight to tickle your hunger for learning or to have something neat to share with your small group. And never study and pray without God's help. He is the one who revealed his truth, and only he can enlighten your mind to know it.[2] He is the one who teaches us to pray when we don't know what to say.[3] Ask him to open his mind and will to you, so that you may know him and love him more. He delights to do it.

3. Meditate on your self in the Word and with God. The power of this meditation and prayer lies in its ability to expose the secret workings of sin—what advantages the flesh has gotten over you, what temptations it has used with success, what harm it has already caused, and what harm it still plans. This prayer and meditation calls on the Spirit to use his Word to shine light into the cracks and crevices of your soul, to show you every real need and danger there.

Without these, *prayer is not prayer.* Without these purposes and longings, your prayers and meditations won't bring any glory to God, and they won't make you holy or fill you with joy.

But with these, prayer and meditation sound the depths of your soul, dredge up the schemes and plots of the law of sin, and drag them into the light of God's presence. In his light every imagination of the flesh is judged, condemned, abhorred, and mourned. "Then," God says through Isaiah,

> you will defile your idols overlaid with silver and your images covered with gold; you will throw them away like a menstrual cloth and say to them, "Away with you!" (Isaiah 30:22)

The Wounded Beast

Suppose your Biology 101 professor handed you a live wolverine and asked you to dissect it—but you had no anesthetic and no way to tie the beast down. What if you talked nicely to the wolverine: "Now, sir, if you just sit still, I'll try to get this over as quickly as possible"? All you'd see would be bare teeth and flying claws in violent resistance to your experiment.

Your flesh won't sit still for meditation and prayer any more than a wolverine would submit to your surgery. The flesh resists with its last breath anything that smacks of communion with God, because it suffocates in his presence. If you draw close to God in meditation and prayer, adoring God, getting to know him, and calling on him to search your heart, prepare to see the flesh scratch and claw like a wounded badger. It will do everything to stop you from meditation and prayer. Here are four claws you can expect to see:

The first claw aims at your weakness. When they were
under attack and in great danger of temptation, just when
they should have been praying, Jesus' disciples were fast
asleep. "The spirit is willing, but the body is weak," he said
(Matthew 26:41). The spiritual flesh takes advantage of the
weakness of the natural flesh (the body). "You can't pray
now, you need your rest. If you don't get some sleep, you
won't be any use to God." This, in effect, is what Satan hit
Jesus with when his body was weakened by forty days of fasting: "You've done enough fasting—you're being downright
fanatical. Turn these stones to bread. If you don't eat, you'll
die, and then how will you save the world!" (Matthew 4:1–3).

If you don't imbed it in your mind that prayer and meditation are indispensable, and seek God's grace every day to
resist the sluggishness of your body, you will hit the snooze
button all morning rather than kneel before the throne.
And if you snooze, you lose.

The second claw is the tyranny of the urgent. "If you
take this praying and meditating business too seriously, you
won't be respected on the job as a hard worker, and you
won't have enough time to spend with other people." The
twisted logic of the flesh is subtle—or it wouldn't work. It
sounds reasonable. It knows that God has called you to work
hard at your calling, and to give yourself to other people in
love. Of course, the flesh would rather you did nothing
noble and pleasing to God; but if it can use your work and
social life to undermine your communion with God, it will.

But think through this: Is it likely that God would call
you to do more than he gives you time to do? No one who

believes God is good and wise could answer yes. So when it seems you don't have enough time to do your work, care for your family, love your friends, *and* devote yourself to prayer and meditation, the problem isn't God's providence. The problem may be that you've taken on yourself more than God intended.

Whatever the problem is, the flesh takes advantage of the opportunity: when there isn't enough time for everything, something has to go. The flesh argues that you can't let your work go, because you have a responsibility to your employer (and if you don't do your best you won't get a raise); you can't take any time away from your family—God would never want that; and of course you shouldn't slight your friends, especially if they're unbelievers, because you may offend them and turn them off to the gospel. So what gets the axe? The very things that will do the flesh the most damage.[4]

The third claw is the duty swap. The desperation of the flesh will argue that if you pray with your family, or if you go to public worship, that's enough spirituality to hold anyone; you can get by without the private, soul-searching prayer and meditation. If you buy that argument, you're sunk.

The fourth claw is the big promise. "You can pray and meditate next week, after you get past your physics mid-term (or the year-end report at work, or landscaping your backyard). You'll be more diligent and faithful then, once you get over this hurdle." Right. This is the cheer of the perennial loser: "We'll get 'em next year!"

The Seeds of Sin

When the watchman fails, not only is he lost, but the whole city is laid waste. When the mind surrenders its watch over the soul by neglecting its duties, the affections and will are sure to follow. Do you think the kind of meditation and prayer described here are too hard to keep up day after day? Remember that "God did not give us a spirit of timidity, but a spirit of power, of love and of *self-discipline*" (2 Timothy 1:7). Hold before your mind the rewards God promises: "My dear brothers, stand firm. Let nothing move you. Always give yourselves fully to the work of the Lord, because you know that your labor in the Lord is not in vain" (1 Corinthians 15:58). And never forget the warning about dropping your guard: "Be on your guard so that you may not be carried away by the error of lawless men and fall from your secure position" (2 Peter 3:17).

God has given you a hammer that crushes the flesh.

> Jes' listen to de col' steel ring,
> Lawd, Lawd, jes' listen to de col' steel ring.

Questions for Reflection and Discussion

1. Consider several examples of meditating on God with God, such as Exodus 15:1–8 and Psalms 8, 135, 138, 145–50. You may also look at some hymns or poems that dwell on God's beauty and adore him. Then write a prayer of your own (at least one paragraph) that asks for nothing, that only admires and revels in God.

2. Bible study is easy to depersonalize. Spend some time reading and praying through Psalm 119, looking for the heart of the true student of the Word. Why does he love God's law (Word)? Why does he long for it? How can you nurture the same attitude in your Bible study?

3. Think about the first temptation of Christ in the wilderness—to turn stones into bread (Matthew 4). The sin proposed to him was to set aside spiritual duty (the Spirit had led him into the desert to fast and pray) and give preference to his physical needs. In what ways are you tempted to put the physical above the spiritual? What makes such temptation so powerful?

4. Meditate on your self with God in his Word. Do you pray fervently and meditate on God in his Word? Do you search the Scriptures in order to know Christ? Has spiritual decay set in? Has your mind, in one way or another, shirked its duty?

excursus | *loving god with all your mind*

Now, here, you see, it takes all the running you can do,
to keep in the same place. If you want to get somewhere else,
you must run at least twice as fast as that!
—Lewis Carroll
Through the Looking-Glass

In chapter 5 I introduced the idea of the flesh's deceit and said we would follow the trail of James 1:14–15 through

(1)   the dragging away of the mind from its duties,
(2)   the entangling of the affections,
(3)   the capturing of the will in consent to sin.

I've already put you through two chapters on the mind, and now I'm taking you on an excursion deeper into the mind's duties. Yet there will be only one chapter each on the affections and the will. Why?

1. Guarding your mind is essential to obedience. Consider Hebrews 2:1:

We must pay more careful attention, therefore, to what we have heard, so that we do not drift away.

The sense of the warning is that we need to give earnest attention to the things we have heard (in the Scriptures), because if we don't, we'll lose the life, power, sense, and impression of them in our minds. There is no way to keep the impression of the Word in our minds except by *constant* care.

2. The mind includes the conscience. If the conscience isn't pricked and stirred up at the sight of sin, it can't help us—and if the mind is dull and led astray, the conscience will be sluggish, or even bribed or corrupted. In Hebrews 5:14 the intense study of the things of Christ leads to a robust, obedient conscience:

> Solid food [the meat of the Scriptures] is for the mature, who *by constant use* have trained themselves to distinguish good from evil.

Thinking Hard About Obedience

To please God with obedience, it isn't enough to merely do *what* he says. The *way* we do it has to square with God's rule. The great duty of the mind is to attend to the *rule* of duties.

Your growth in obedience is a house you build. You can't build a house you'd want to live in by heaping up bricks and wood without order. You have to cut and square and fit everything according to a plan. In the same way, you won't grow in obedience if you merely pile up duties one on the other, not according to God's rule.

> "The multitude of your sacrifices—
>> what are they to me?" says the LORD.
> "I have more than enough of burnt offerings,
>> of rams and the fat of fattened animals;
> I have no pleasure
>> in the blood of bulls and lambs and goats.
>> . . .
> Your New Moon festivals and your appointed
>> feasts
>> my soul hates.
> They have become a burden to me;
>> I am weary of bearing them." (Isaiah 1:11, 14)

Words mean nothing unless they are arranged according to the rules of language. Duties piled up mean nothing to God unless they are done according to his rule. The work of your mind is to know his rule and apply it to all you do before God, to "be very careful, then, how you live" (or, in the King James Version, to "walk circumspectly"—Ephesians 5:15).

God wants us to think deeply about what pleases him (verse 10). These are some of the duties of the mind for everything that pleases God:

1. Obey fully. Under the Old Testament ceremonial law no animal could be a sacrifice unless it was completely free of spot or defect. Similarly, duties must be complete in all their parts—nothing lacking. When Saul spared Agag, he did not perform his duty in every part (1 Samuel 15). The mind must study to know everything that pleases God.

2. Obey by faith. Every duty must be done in faith, in the strength from Christ. Apart from him we can do nothing (John 15:5). It isn't enough for you to be a believer, though that's the beginning of every good work (Ephesians 2:10)— you must also act in faith in every duty. Our whole obedience is "the obedience that comes from faith" (Romans 1:5). So Christ is called "our life" (Colossians 3:4), meaning he is our spiritual life: the spring, Author, and cause of it. No spiritually living act—no duty that is acceptable to God—can be performed but by the actual working of Christ, who is our life. "The life I live in the body, I live by faith in the Son of God" (Galatians 2:20).

3. Obey from the heart. In the next chapter we'll see in detail how the affections either cling to God or get entangled in sin, but now we're looking at how the mind must watch over the affections in every duty to God. A duty offered to God as an act of mind and will without the affections is abominable to God. A duty without spiritual affections is a sacrifice without fire—worthless, unacceptable. "God loves a cheerful giver," not merely someone who grudgingly drops money in the plate.

4. Obey God's way. Your mind has to make sure you do everything the way and by the means God has commanded.

He has commanded us, for example, to worship him. But how? Are we free to make up ways to worship him? No. We must worship him in spirit and in *truth*—according to his directions for worship, which we find in the Word and not in our imagination.

5. Obey God for God's goals. Your mind must search out the purpose of every duty, the main goal always being the glory of God in Christ. If your mind sleeps on its watch here, the flesh will try to slip in other motivations for your obedience, such as satisfying your conscience or winning the praise of your peers. If the flesh succeeds, it ruins your obedience. "Whatever you do, do it all to the glory of God" (1 Corinthians 10:31).

The Flesh's Counteroffensive

The minute you engage your mind to please the Lord, you'll find the flesh resisting every thought. Here are his top three ways to short-circuit holy thinking:

1. Don't get specific. The flesh wants your mind to be content to think in general about what pleases God. For example, sin tries to persuade your mind to be happy with having a general aim of doing things to the glory of God, without ever considering particular ways to glorify God in your marriage or your work or in a conversation. But if you want to visit your cousin in Longview, you can't just head in the general direction of Texas; you have to pay attention to every turn—or you may wander on and fall into the Gulf of

Mexico. Our *particular* actions express and exercise our faith and obedience. And what we are in faith and obedience, that we are, and nothing more.

2. Be content with naked duty. Israel expected God to be pleased with them because they went through the motions of fasting.

> "Why have we fasted," they say,
>   "and you have not seen it?
> Why have we humbled ourselves,
>   and you have not noticed?" (Isaiah 58:3)

They had the idea that if they did what God said (at least with their bodies) and satisfied him, then they could run on and do whatever they *really* wanted to do.

> Yet on the day of your fasting, you do as you
>   please
> and exploit all your workers. (verse 3)

The deceitfulness of the flesh says, "You ought to pray, so pray; you ought to tithe, so tithe; now you've done your duty, so go and do what you want."

3. Get into a routine. The ultimate success of the flesh is to get you to obey perfunctorily. Your mind is completely dragged away from its duty when you can go to worship Sunday after Sunday, say your prayers day after day, pile duty after duty up into a great heap—yet never offer a single acceptable act of obedience to God, because you're just going through the motions. This kind of "Christian" life isn't lived for God, no matter what you say.

> Did you bring me sacrifices and offerings
>> forty years in the desert, O house of Israel?
> You have lifted up the shrine of your king,
>> the pedestal of your idols,
>> the star of your god—
> which you made for yourselves.
>> (Amos 5:25–26)

Thinking Hard About Sin

One of the means God has given us to overcome the power and deceit of the law of sin in us is to put our minds to work not just *for* obedience, but *against* sin. These are some ways you can use your head to weaken the flesh.

1. Think about the sovereignty of God. Think about the great Lawgiver who forbids sin. This helped keep Joseph out of bed with Potiphar's wife (Genesis 39:9). Consider this always: There is only one Lawgiver, holy and righteous, armed with sovereign power and authority; he is able to save and destroy. Sin is rebellion—throwing off the rule and sovereignty of the Lawgiver. When you come face to face with the lust of the flesh, think, *It is God who forbids this; the great Lawgiver, who rules in sovereignty over me, on whom I depend for every breath of life, and from whom I can expect my lot in this life and the next.*

2. *Think about the punishment of sin.* Even when God declares his gracious name to encourage poor sinners in Christ, he adds that "he will by no means let the guilty go unpunished" (Exodus 34:7). He wants to keep in the mind of everyone he pardons a deep sense of the punishment every sin deserves. Keep in mind that "our God is a consuming fire" (Hebrews 10:29). To forget this or ignore this is to slap God in the face (Romans 1:32). Jesus counseled us to fear him "who can destroy both body and soul in hell" (Matthew 10:28).

> For we know him who said, "It is mine to avenge; I will repay," and again, "The Lord will judge his people." It is a dreadful thing to fall into the hands of the living God. (Hebrews 10:30–31)

3. *Think about all the love and kindness of God, against whom every sin is committed.* When God's love touches your soul and moves you, and you know that every sin is against the Lover of your soul, you will not sin.

> Is this the way you repay the LORD,
>   O foolish and unwise people?
> Is he not your Father, your Creator,
>   who made you and formed you?
>   (Deuteronomy 32:6)

Paul says that "since we have these promises, dear friends, let us purify ourselves from everything that contaminates body and spirit, perfecting holiness out of reverence for God" (2 Corinthians 7:1). What kind of promises motivate this purity? Look at 2 Corinthians 6:17–18:

> "Therefore come out from them
>> and be separate,"
>>> says the Lord.
> "Touch no unclean thing,
>> and I will receive you.
> I will be a Father to you,
>> and you will be my sons and daughters,"
>>> says the Lord Almighty.

When you think about God's love, think first about God's *general* love to all believers (1 John 3:1–3). Consider the love of God, the privileges of it, the fruit of it—how it is so great the world cannot know it—in fact, we can't fathom the greatness of it. When you relish this love, you will purify yourself, even as he is pure.

But don't stop with God's general love. Go on to dwell on his *particular love to you.* Think of his mercy to you for particular sins, the way he has delivered you from temptations, how he has provided for you and protected you, all he has taught you. To fail to consider God's particular love provokes him.

> The LORD became angry with Solomon because his heart had turned away from the LORD, the God of Israel, *who had appeared to him twice.* (1 Kings 11:9)

4. Think about the blood and mediation of Christ.

For Christ's love compels us, because we are convinced that one died for all, and therefore all died. And he died for all, that those who live should no longer live for themselves but for him who died for them and was raised again. (2 Corinthians 5:14–15)

5. Think about the indwelling of the Holy Spirit—the greatest privilege we are made partakers of in this world. If you fully consider how sin grieves the Spirit, how it defiles his dwelling place, how you lose and forfeit his comforts by it—this works against the lusting of sin.

The Flesh's Counteroffensive

In order to defend itself, the law of sin uses its deceit to drag the mind away from these powerful thoughts by making us *spiritually lazy.*

The main command the Lord Jesus gives us in order to prevent sin and temptation is to *watch* (Mark 13:37). To "watch" means to be diligent to not be surprised and entangled by temptations (see Deuteronomy 32:29; Hebrews 6:11–12; 2 Peter 1:5–11). You know that you've fallen into spiritual laziness when you aren't stirred by warnings against sin, when you can't be motivated to spiritual duty, and when you are easily discouraged and give up at the sight of difficulties. A lazy soul realizes he'll never be perfect, so he says, "Why bother?" and is content with spiritual deadness and apathy.

Questions for Reflection and Discussion

1. What is the place of the mind in obeying God? Why is it such a target of the flesh's deceit?

2. What is your gut-level reaction to the extensive list of duties of the mind in this excursus—does it seem like a delight or a burden to you? What could make it seem more delightful?

3. What does it mean to obey *in faith*? Choose a duty (such as public worship, tithing, or showing mercy to the poor) and write a description of how to perform that duty in faith. What role does the mind play?

4. Examine your heart, asking the Holy Spirit's help (Psalm 139:23–24). Ask him in particular what your motives most often are for doing your spiritual duty. Depending on what you find, give thanks or repent.

5. Look back to the times in your life when you have been hungriest to search out the things of God, especially to "find out what pleases the Lord" (Ephesians 5:10). What was motivating you then? What turned your mind on to God? Was it sermons you heard? Something you read in the Scriptures? Encouragement from a mentor or a small group? What was it?

6. What one or two duties of the mind from this chapter do you most need to learn and give your mind to? What makes them stand out to you?

8 | *hooked*

And when the timorous Trout I wait
To take, and he devours my bait,
How poor a thing, sometimes I find,
Will captivate a greedy mind. . . .
—Izaak Walton

The Flesh Goes Fishing

James must have been, like most of his Brother's other followers, an old angler. When he wrote that we are tempted when we are "dragged away and *enticed*" (James 1:14), he used fishing lingo. On the shores of the Sea of Galilee the word translated "enticed" meant "caught by bait." It's a suggestive image of the way the flesh hooks our affections.

Even if you aren't a veteran angler, you know that if you simply drop a naked hook in the water you aren't likely to catch anything. The hook has to be covered, disguised, made to look attractive to the kind of fish you want to catch. It has to be decorated by a worm or a fly or a spinner or a plug. It has to be desirable, attractive, *alluring*. The bait doesn't just invite—it *seduces*.

James says that the flesh is a "fisher of men." It deceives

and seduces us with temptation. It dangles the pleasures of sin in front of us (Hebrews 11:25), decorating those supposed delights until they look like something to sell your soul for—until you can hardly see the hook they hide. The sparkling bubbles of wine advertise taste, sophistication, social acceptance, forgetting your troubles—but they hide a bitter self-destruction (see Proverbs 23:29–35). The loose woman promises secret pleasures without fear of discovery—but her rose-strewn bed is your lily-covered grave (Proverbs 7).[1]

The design of these trappings is to entangle the affections by catching your imagination. The imagination is the mind's eye. With the imagination we paint and contemplate pictures of how things might be. You can imagine yourself doing things that aren't (yet) real: getting a call from Ed McMahon that your $10,000,000 check is in the mail, catching a pass in the corner of the end-zone at the gun to win the Super Bowl, putting one boyfriend on hold because another boy is calling on the other line. The flesh wants to fix your imagination on something that will lead you into the clutches of sin. It wants you to dwell on and savor those tantalizing possibilities, until you can't stop thinking about them, until you start plotting and scheming ways to make the fantasy a reality.

This is why Paul warns us not even to "think about how to gratify the desires of the flesh" (Romans 13:14). Those with "eyes full of adultery" (2 Peter 2:14) are like Augustine before his conversion, unable to stomach the thought of a night without a lover.[2] His imagination was so entangled in his lust that he couldn't stop sinning (verse 14). Such people "plot evil on their beds," which they carry out in the morning (Micah 2:1). Once the affections are enticed, the will soon follows with its happy consent.

An amazing thing about this seduction is that the flesh can never completely hide the hook from the sinner. We always know deep inside that the "wages of sin is death" (Romans 6:23), even when we plunge into evil (Romans 1:32). But the flesh succeeds when it makes you forget or ignore or not care about the hook whose dim outline you see beneath the feathers and flash of the lure. The flesh makes you careless of the hook by promising that you'll be pardoned later. It ambushes you with sudden, overpowering temptation so that you have no time to think about consequences. It pleads extenuating circumstances: "This is *true* love, not some trashy infatuation—a loving God would *never* condemn something so beautiful—and we plan to get married when the time is right." Or it tempts you to think that your generous gifts to the church in the last year have more than balanced this little oversight on your income tax return.

Disguising the danger of sin under delicious decorations—this is how the flesh hooks your affections.

You Know You've Been Hooked When . . .

The biggest buzzword in leadership seminars nowadays is *vision*. Powerful leaders compel followers by their ability to paint vivid pictures of a desirable future—a future that can only become real if you follow their plan. When Bill Gates describes a world with a computer on every desk, so that a Thai farmer can be linked on the Internet to his banker in Bern and his cousin's restaurant in Orange County, and you can turn in your feasibility study, finish your Christmas shopping, and deposit your paycheck all with a few keystrokes on your laptop as you sit in bed—a lot of people are turned on. They'll buy Bill's software and follow his program if in return they'll live on the convenient planet he promises.

The power of vision comes from the imagination—the leader imagining paradise, then helping others to imagine it with him. He whets their appetite, and when they see it clearly, and when it looks good enough, they'll do anything to make it happen, because their affections hunger for it.

The flesh has a vision of its own. It sees a world free from the tyranny of God's rule. It imagines the liberty to carry out all its plans without interference from law, precept, or command. And it proposes that vision to your imagination, helping you to see the juicy possibilities: Remember how your manager fired you not two weeks after giving you that glowing performance review? Imagine how gratifying it would be to help him suffer a little. Wouldn't it ease your rage to take your utility knife to his valve stems, so he wakes up to four flat tires on the morning he's supposed to be at a meeting with the vice president of research? Or how about a little note to his wife, clueing her in to what her hubby really does on those business trips to Manitou Springs? Imagine how gratifying it would be to read in the paper that she filed for divorce.

When your imagination can't turn off the flesh's images of evil, you're hooked. When you can't stop thinking about how Bill, the new guy in marketing, respects you so much more than your husband of seven years, you're hooked. When you stay up late every night trying to balance your budget, and always end up toying with the idea of cutting your tithe in half, you're hooked. When your wife has been asking for a sewing table for 18 years, and you've always put it off because you couldn't justify the extravagant expense, yet every evening on the way home you slow down as you pass the Mazda dealer and imagine yourself in the British-racing-green Miata convertible, guess what?[3]

Achan "saw in the plunder a beautiful robe from Babylonia" (Joshua 7:21), and he couldn't stop thinking about how good he'd look in that robe, so he took it. This is the "lust of the eyes" (1 John 2:16)—not just the physical eyes, but the mind's eye that fixes itself on something forbidden until the affections are consumed by desire for it.

Remember that the mind is the watchman of the soul. Its duty is to discern and judge what words, actions, desires, thoughts, beliefs, and emotions will please the Lord. The affections, when they are working as they should, long for and cling to what the mind says is pleasing to God, and are repulsed by what angers him. When you "harbor wicked thoughts" (Jeremiah 4:14), the imagination becomes a pyromaniac dumping buckets of gasoline on the fire of your affections. They burn hotter and hotter, till the will melts like butter before them.

But you protest, "I might *think* about those things, but I'd never *do* them." You may be firmly convinced that you would be the last person in the world to give your body away before marriage. You've memorized the Ten Commandments, and know how immorality brought down the strongest man in the world, the wisest man who ever lived, and the man who loved God more than anyone ever has.[4] But if you think it's okay to *daydream* about inviting your boyfriend over for the night while your parents are out of town, and to imagine how grown up you'd feel and how you could finally be yourselves together, as long as you don't actually *do* it, your convictions will go on vacation with Mom and Dad.

Don't Get Caught

Most of us wouldn't bend over to pick up a penny. But if you have eight new hundred-dollar bills on you, you might move your wallet to your front pocket, or carry your purse with your hand over the opening. We guard most closely what we most treasure.

Solomon, out of his painful experience, pleaded with his children,

> Above all else, guard your heart,
>> for it is the wellspring of life.
> (Proverbs 4:23)

What is it you most protect? Your reputation? Your investments? Your family? Of all you guard, says Solomon, guard nothing with the care and strength you guard your affections. Once your heart latches onto something, you will not be able to stop your will from consenting to it.[5]

To protect your affections, you need to be careful of two things: the *object* of your affections, and the *vigor* of your affections. And the object of your affections, what you fix your eyes on, should always be heavenly things: "Set your minds on things above, not on earthly things" (Colossians 3:2). Fix your affections on God himself, in his beauty and glory. Fix your heart on the Lord Christ, the fairest of ten thousand, the desired of the nations. Get worked up about the mystery of the gospel, all the wisdom and love of God displayed in Christ, and all the blessings he delivers to your soul. If you're going to revel in and relish something, be like Paul:

> May I never boast except in the cross of our Lord Jesus Christ, through which the world has been crucified to me, and I to the world. (Galatians 6:14)

Let the sorrows of your Savior on the cross move you. Imagine his cries and groans in your behalf, till your heart breaks. Daydream about how much love he showed you as he hung naked in your place. And see if the baits and lures of the flesh don't grow ugly and repulsive. Will you give your hours to fantasizing about and dwelling on and longing for the vile things that nailed the Lover of your soul to the cursed tree?

Set your heart on heavenly things, especially the cross—and be careful to keep your affections warm.[6] There is a moral gravity that will drag down and weaken your affections for Christ unless you constantly stir them up. How many Christians have forsaken their first love because they have let their hearts grow slowly cooler?

Fill your affections with the cross of Christ, and there will be no room for sin. Then, when the flesh fishes for your affections, you'll spit on its pretty lures.

> And when none bite, I praise the wise
> Whom vain allurements ne'er surprise.[7]

Questions for Reflection and Discussion

1. We tend to think of fantasies as sexual, but the imagination can be filled with all sorts of good or evil, including ambition, hatred, revenge, and greed. Are you a daydreamer? Where is your mind most likely to wander during a dull lecture or late-afternoon staff meeting? Do you have a recurring fantasy?

2. Suppose you wanted to convince your child that imagining evil, even if you don't intend to carry it out, is dangerous. How would you build your case? What Scriptures would you use? How would you help your child overcome destructive daydreaming?

3. How often do you fantasize about the resurrection? Reigning with Christ forever (Revelation 22:5)? In worship do you ever imagine that you are joining your voice to the saints in heaven (Hebrew 12:22–23)? Should such things fill your heart? If they don't, what can you do to make them your daydreams?

4. From the standpoint of Christ's humanity, what role do you think his imagination played in his obedience to God? (See Hebrews 12:2–3 for a possible suggestion.) Is there a parallel role that your imagination should play in your obedience? What is it?

5. What is it about the relationship between the imagination and the affections that makes the imagination so important to guard?

9 | *maculate conception*

A little still she strove, and much repented,
And whispering "I will ne'er consent!"—consented.
—Lord Byron

Excuse Me?

"I was only following orders."

"I didn't know the gun was loaded."

"The Devil made me do it."

We often try to excuse our unwelcome behavior by attributing our work to the command of some higher-ups, by pleading ignorance, or by arguing an outward coercion or compulsion that robbed us of freedom. Though most such self-absolutions are dubious, they rely on a universally accepted fact: we can only be blamed (or credited) for something we did willingly, or with consent. Anything you say or do or think or feel can only be sinful to the degree you say or do or think or feel it willingly.

The consent of the will completes the flesh's seduction of the soul. The mind is dragged away from its duty as watchman, the affections are enticed and entangled, the will says "I do," and sin is conceived.[1] Unless God in his providence aborts the embryonic sin, it will be born into the world and bear its deadly fruit.[2]

Two Kinds of Consent

"You want to pay my way to Italy and put me up in a five-star hotel in Florence for a month? Of course I'll go!"

"You want me to go with you to the cock-fights Friday night at 3:00 A.M., and then chow down at the gut-buster breakfast buffet at Golden Corral? Frankly, I've never delighted to watch birds mutilate each other, but since you went to *The Marriage of Figarro* with me last week, I'll go."

Consent of the will is a tricky thing. Sometimes we give our consent to something freely, fully, absolutely, after careful deliberation. Sometimes we consent reluctantly to "the lesser of two evils." Sometimes we do something on impulse that we immediately regret and can't explain. Consent becomes downright mysterious when it gets to the point that you can say with Paul, "What I want to do I do not do, but what I hate, I do" (Romans 7:15). We need to make a distinction in order to sort this out.

Let's distinguish two kinds of consent to sin:

Sins of the high hand. In Ephesians 4:19 Paul speaks of those who have "given themselves over to sensuality so as to indulge in every kind of impurity, with a continual lust for more." Such consent to sin is full, absolute, complete, and with deliberation. With this consent the soul plunges into sin like a ship at full sail with the wind at its back. This is the kind of consent that unbelievers give to sin and isn't what we need to think about.

Sins of the willy-nilly. When believers consent to sin, there is always a secret reluctance. In Galatians 5:17 we find out that not only does the flesh war against the Spirit, but the Spirit in us wars against the flesh. The Spirit in us is grieved by our sin and can't delight in it. Since the believer is born of the sin-hating Spirit, he can never give himself to sin fully, absolutely, the way an unbeliever can. The believer's consent is like a ship sailing against the wind—the wind may be stiff or light, perhaps even hardly felt, but it is always there in the believer's renewed heart, resisting the consent to sin.

When Peter denied the Master, he did what he was no longer capable of.[3] There was something inside him that hated what he was doing. When he heard the rooster crow, that something burst into tears. Yes, he sinned willingly; but even as he swore "I don't know him!" and called down curses on himself, he loved Jesus and his faith never completely failed.

This secret reluctance in the believer isn't simply a general opposition to sin as a bad thing. In every individual sinful thought, word, action, or feeling, God's grace fights against the will's consent. Just as the flesh resists every spiritual act, the Spirit resists every sin. The wisdom of the believer is to learn to listen to the voice of the Spirit's resistance, no matter how faintly it may echo in the conscience. The folly of the believer is to ignore that voice repeatedly, until he becomes nearly deaf to it. This is greasing the tracks for sin.

Passive Consent Is Real Consent

Suppose my friend Stanley is getting ready to spend a few months in the Central African Republic. Dr. Livingston tells him he must take a series of inoculations, or he will certainly get malaria. Stan looks into it and finds the pills will cost him $200, so he balks. Four months later Stan is on his deathbed, looking up at Dr. Livingston's I-told-you-so face.

Who is responsible for Stan's sickness (and perhaps death)? Is it Dr. Livingston, since he didn't coerce Stanley into taking the pills? Is it the hospital's fault for price-gouging? Is it the mosquitoes' fault? Of course not. Stan was warned. He knew what he had to do in order to prevent malaria. But he chose, because of the cost, not to take the pills. He has no one to blame but himself.

God has made it clear to us what we must do in order to defeat sin:

> For if you live according to the flesh you will die; but if by the Spirit you put to death the misdeeds of the body, you will live. (Romans 8:13)

The Great Physician has warned us. Killing the flesh is expensive (it will cost us much work and time, though aided by the Spirit), but the alternative is spiritual death. Those who refuse to put the flesh to death are willing to live according to the flesh. This is consent to sin. So it is not necessary to plan to murder or lust or steal or lie in order to give your consent to sin. All you have to do is willingly neglect the means God has given to put an end to sin.

Persuasion

God created the will so that it only chooses what it believes to be good for or agreeable to the soul—or at least better for or more agreeable to the soul than other options.[4] That's easy to understand when someone chooses chocolate mousse for dessert over the peaches in brandy if he has violent allergic reactions to peaches. It's still easy to see it when someone who hates broccoli eats it anyway because she knows it's good for her. But what about the person who freely chooses to drink grape Kool-Aid laced with arsenic, knowing it will kill him?

Even the person who blows his own brains out in despair has chosen what he was convinced is "good"—"it is better to die and face what's on the other side than to go on living like this." This fundamental principle of the will is the basis of everything the flesh does in order to seduce us. All the deception and temptation we've been discussing has one intent: to convince the mind that this sinful act is somehow "good" for the soul so that the affections hunger for it, and the will chooses it.

The ways the flesh does this are countless. Here are just a few to guard against.

Twisted Scripture. First John 2:1 describes both the design of the gospel, that we be holy, and the relief promised when we fall:

> My dear children, I write this [about the work of Christ; see 1 John 1:2] to you so that you will not sin.

But if anybody does sin, we have one who speaks to the Father in our defense—Jesus Christ, the Righteous One.

If the flesh can persuade you to consider only the second sentence of 1 John 2:1, the temptation to sin is almost a piece of cake. If your mind sees the gospel only as a source of pardon from sin, and not also as the source of deliverance from the power of sin, you will be more easily attracted by the pleasures of sin, convinced that any threats of danger have been carried away in Christ. The flesh will have you singing its corrupted gospel theme song,

> Saved by grace—
> Oh blessed condition!
> I can sin all I want
> and still have remission!

The double standard. "How could anything that feels so right be so wrong?" The flesh will rarely try to convince a believer that adultery in general is right—that is, that God's seventh commandment was just a joke. But it is repeatedly successful in making believers think that this particular instance of sleeping with your secretary is okay, perhaps even beautiful to God, because it is "true love," and your marriage to your wife never should have happened in the first place.[5]

The idea is to make your case exceptional—I don't have to report this cash income to the IRS because it is an evil organization, or because it is only a few hundred dollars (and what is that compared to what corporations steal from the government every day?), or so that I can have more money to give to the church. It's okay for me to spend half my time at work on The Internet Gaming Zone playing spades with people in London and Tokyo because I still meet my deadlines.

Keeping you in the dark. Sin loves darkness. A mind ignorant of God's commands, or downright wrong about what God wants, will stumble and fall as surely as a man climbing El Capitan on a moonless night.

Though our minds have been renewed in Christ, some darkness remains (1 Corinthians 13:12), and the flesh takes advantage of that. If we neglect the Word of Christ—the lamp for our path (Psalm 119:105)—we'll grope and stumble in the dark.

The flesh wins countless victories by keeping souls in the dark about what God requires of them on the Sabbath, or convincing them that the law has been done away with in Christ. How many fathers, ignorant of their duty to disciple and train their children by personal involvement in their lives (Deuteronomy 6:4–9), leave their whole Christian training up to the Sunday school teacher or the youth group leader, only to see them turn from the faith as adults?

"Find out what pleases the Lord" (Ephesians 5:10).

Don't worry about it. The flesh knows that the means of grace will ruin its hard work. It knows that if you meditate and pray and seek God's pleasure, calling on the Spirit, living in faith and reliance on God, you'll weaken and eventually crush sin's power. So its work includes persuading you to ignore the Word and Spirit. You should be suspicious when you hear a voice in your head whisper, *This sin isn't that bad—you don't need to go to all that trouble against this little thing. Other Christians, even great saints in the Bible, have committed far more grievous sins than yours, yet God forgave them. Don't worry about it—everything will work out okay in the end.*

No More Excuses

We've looked at the power and deception of the law of sin that remains even in believers. We've seen its mortal hatred of God, and its unscrupulous trickery to turn you against your Lord. Can there be an ounce of indifference left in you? Can you possibly think the flesh is something to ignore, or even to toy with?

Questions for Reflection and Discussion

1. What is the most bizarre excuse you've ever given to justify something you had done wrong? Did it work? What motivated you to make up the excuse, and what made you think it would work?

2. What do you think about the section on "Passive Consent"? Do you agree that consenting to lay aside the means to kill sin is consent to sin? What means of defeating sin have you learned (if any) from this book? How will you take them up in battle against sin?

3. Although it's true that the new life of the Spirit in us resists every work of the flesh (Galatians 5:17), some-

times we don't sense the struggle. What could make a believer oblivious to the war in his own soul?

4. Pick a sin that, when you are thinking clearly, is obviously egregious (something like cold-blooded murder, lying under oath in federal hearings, or insurance fraud). Describe the process the flesh might use to make a specific sin sound justifiable to your soul. Use as much detail as you can.

5. Suppose your child got hold of some bad theology, being persuaded that Jesus came only to forgive his sins, not to make him holy. What Scriptures and scriptural arguments would you use to convince him or her of this error? Write a letter to your child about this (and save it, just in case).

6. Since the flesh uses our ignorance of what God requires of us in order to settle us in sin, what are our responsibilities to learn God's will and pleasure? How does this affect the way you study the Scriptures?

part three

The Power of Sin in What It Does

Security
Is mortals' chiefest enemy.
—Shakespeare
Macbeth

10 | *slip-sliding away*

. . . deep as love,
Deep as first love, and wild with all regret;
O Death in Life, the days that are no more.
—Alfred, Lord Tennyson

Just How Tough Is the Flesh, Anyway?

Michael Jordan can play basketball. Suppose we want to find out how good Michael *really* is. How can we test him? It wouldn't prove much to see if he could take Richard Simmons one-on-one. But we could blindfold him during a game, or put 15-pound weights on his wrists and ankles, or let the three best defenders in basketball guard him at all times. What if we did all three, yet Michael still hit his fade-aways, still exploded through the lane for tongue-wagging monster dunks, still nailed back-breaking three pointers? No one would ever again doubt that he's the best ever.

Now suppose we need to know just how tough the flesh is. How can we test it? It wouldn't prove much to see if it could make the Marquis de Sade stumble into sin. But we could pit him against someone who was a man after God's heart, someone head and shoulders above others in his holiness and zeal for God. Someone like David. But let's really test the flesh—let's not make it David when he's a young man into high-risk behavior, before he's had much experience walking with God: let's make it David after decades of tasting the sweetness of God, years of practiced obedience, even after many experiences of the power and deceit of sin itself. And let's not make it David after some great disappointment in life, but David on the heels of God's mercy, after he's seen God deliver all his enemies into his hands. If *this* David spots a woman bathing on a nearby roof and dives into adultery, lying, and murder, we should never again doubt the power of the flesh.

But if you still doubt the power of the flesh, let's put it to a stiffer test: God's people under the new covenant. How will the flesh fare against people who have the whole written revelation of God in the completed Scriptures, and the fulness of the revelation of God in Christ? How will the flesh look when it's set against people who have been given the ministry of the Word as a gift from Jesus (Ephesians 4:11)— a ministry that is designed to bring those people to perfection (verses 12–15)—a ministry that is fit to prepare them against the deceitfulness of sin (verse 13)? Let's give these people more: countless exhortations and warnings from God (Hebrews 2:1), continual supplies of grace flowing from the Fountain of Life himself (Colossians 3:3; Galatians 2:20), life by the Spirit (Romans 8:11), even abundant life (John 10:10). Let's make them children of a generous Father, and brothers of a merciful High Priest who knows their weakness and is always ready to help them in trouble (Hebrews 2:18).

How does the flesh do against *this* great enemy? Could he, for example, get such people to forsake their first love for Christ?

Love on Fire

Remember your honeymoon? Arnold Schwartzenegger couldn't have pried the two of you apart. That's the strength of first love. That's what Solomon sang about: "love is as strong as death. . . . It burns like a blazing fire. . . . rivers cannot wash it away" (Song of Songs 8:6–7). That's the love Jesus cherishes.[1] He hates to lose it. He makes it the model and measure of our love for him so that when we forsake it, we feel his hot wrath and jealous threats breathing down our necks (Revelation 2:4–5; 3:1–3). What makes first love so special to him?

First Love Is Beautiful in Humility

In Luke 7 Jesus was eating at the home of a Pharisee. An immoral woman followed him there, crashed the party, anointed his feet with tears and perfume, and dried them with her hair. Jesus had a few words with his host over this, because the Pharisee despised her. Jesus praised her first love for him when he said that she loved much because she was forgiven much.

Jesus didn't say this adulteress was more wicked than the Pharisee. On the contrary, he had no stronger words of judgment than he did for the self-righteous Pharisees (in Matthew 23, for example). He meant that her great love, which spilled over with tears and tenderness for him, flowed from a clear sight of how much she had wronged God, and how much he had pardoned her.

She looked at her life and saw nothing but emptiness, deceit, and impurity. When Jesus called, she came, baffled that he would want her. She knew God was holy, that he was a consuming fire who could not bear to look at sin. She knew that he was all-powerful, that he could make pure worshipers for himself out of rocks, and that he didn't need praise from her unclean lips. Yet she heard from Jesus that God was merciful, and that out of his sheer mercy, not because she was a lovable or holy person, but because *he* was Love incarnate, he offered to forgive her. So she took hold of him, believed him, and found unspeakable joy.

Her love for him was heated white hot by this fan: a sense of how much God had freely forgiven her in Christ.

The apostle Paul lived such a consistent life as a determined follower of Jesus because he kept this sense his whole life, so that the mercy of Christ compelled him and drove him on. At the end of his life he called himself "The Chief of Sinners" (1 Timothy 1:15 KJV), because he knew how much God had done for him. Fueled daily by new tastes of his own sin and Christ's pardon, his first love burned long and bright.

First Love Is Beautiful in Hunger

In John 6 Jesus delivered some tough teaching. He told the Jews he was the manna that had come from heaven; and he said there was no life in anyone but him. But they thought this was blasphemy, and they had no stomach for him. Many who had been his followers deserted him.

So Jesus turned to the Twelve, and asked them whether they wanted to leave as well. Peter answered for them all and said, "Lord, to whom shall we go? You have the words of eternal life" (John 6:68). Others turned from Christ to look for abundant life in the world. But the Twelve had tasted Jesus, and because they had a taste of spiritual things in Christ, they lost all appetite for things of the world. They knew nothing else could fill their famished souls. They knew that the love of the world and the love of God are like oil and vinegar—they don't mix (Matthew 6:24; 1 John 2:15–17).

A new convert has a fresh taste of the manna from heaven. He finds his desires met in Christ and is satisfied by him. So when the new believer is offered the things of the world, he turns up his nose, convinced that Jesus and Jesus alone is the bread that will feed him.

Seven Cold Splashes on First-Love Fire

If rivers can't wash away the blazes of first love between a man and a woman, what power can cool the passion of first love for the Pearl of Great Price himself? The flesh surely tries to in its war against the Spirit. It hates God and wants us to have nothing to do with him. It especially hates our tasting his grace and mercy. So it dumps seven buckets of ice water on our first love. And its success against the first love of so many Christians takes our breath away.[2]

1. The flesh knows how to eat an elephant. The flesh knows that it wouldn't succeed against us if it stormed the castle and tried to crush our love in one blow. It is subtle, working carefully and deliberately to pick our love apart. The flesh eats away love the way you eat an elephant—one bite at a time.

Indwelling sin takes advantage of our natural laziness and negligence in spiritual things, enticing us to lay aside spiritual duties one by one. It won't at first get God completely out of our minds. But it will talk us into thinking of him less and less, making us think we can get by with a little less prayer, shorter or fewer private devotions—until he at last convinces us that we can get along without talking to God at all.

2. The flesh dresses us up in tuxedoes and evening gowns. If we insist on worshiping God, the flesh will make our religion into a formal affair, so that it has no power. The flesh will let us go through the external motions of spiritual duties, without any fear or reverence for God—so that our worship becomes a stench in God's nostrils. Hebrews 12:28–29 says, "Let us worship God *acceptably* with *reverence* and *awe,* for our God is a consuming fire." God won't accept mere outward worship from us. When we deal with him, he demands our whole heart and soul and mind and strength—not just our bodies, but our thoughts, our longings and dreams, our everything (John 4:23–24). To approach him without fear is to approach him without thinking about who he is: the God of the universe, who holds the nations in his hands, who can create and destroy.[3]

3. The flesh sends us down rabbit trails. In 2 Corinthians 11:2–3 Paul worried that the Corinthians had been deceived and lost their pure devotion to Christ. The flesh wants to sidetrack us from the simplicity of the gospel, so that

Jesus is not our all in all. It steers us toward a religious or political or moral cause as a substitute for passion for him. It entices us to give our lives to the cause as our chief end.

Like the husband who will paint his body the colors of his team and scream his lungs out and high-five his friends at the stadium, then come home from the game and hardly look at his wife, there are many passionate, outspoken activists who never lift their eyes above the cause to see the Christ. They've lost their first love in a swirl of activity.

4. The flesh turns sin into a cuddly pet. Cuddly pets are sins that we domesticate and harbor in our hearts. We think of them as either too small or too great to take to God. Or we just plain get too attached to them to let go. Augustine, before he was converted, was in love with his sensuality. He couldn't bear a night without a lover. As his heart was turning to God, as he felt conviction for his sin, but before he knew what it was to love God, he prayed, "Lord, give me purity—but not yet."[4]

When David prayed in the Psalms about his unconfessed sins, he admitted they crushed him, blinded him so that he couldn't look at God—they festered like untreated wounds and killed his love for God (Psalm 40:12; 38:5). Unrepented and cherished sin douses the fire of first love.

5. The flesh pumps up our heads and shrivels our hearts. "Knowledge puffs up" (1 Corinthians 8:1). When Paul said that to the Corinthians, he wasn't suggesting they stop learning the Word of God. He was condemning knowledge that seems to grow but never moves the heart.

A person with a big head and a small heart can learn the doctrines of sin, yet never be convicted of sin. He can learn the teachings of grace and pardon and the great atonement for sin, yet never feel the peace of God that passes understanding. When the flesh gets a person to the point that he can sit under the teaching of the Word, and even delight in it for its intellectual beauty, yet not be changed, he has snuffed out the wick of his first love.[5]

6. *The flesh gets us to do our own thing.* The flesh tries to put out the fire of our love by gradually persuading us to live according to its wisdom, rather than God's. The wisdom of the flesh is to trust in self (the flesh). God condemns such "wisdom" in Isaiah 47:10: "Your wisdom and knowledge mislead you when you say to yourself, 'I am, and there is none besides me.'" A believer can't sing both "I Love You, Lord" and "I Did It My Way." Independence is the opposite of faith and love. Faith and love trust another; the flesh's self-trust douses the fire of first love.

7. *The flesh is a cat that gets our tongue.* The greatest destroyer of first-love fire is the neglect of private communion with God. In Isaiah 43:22 God says, "You have not called upon me, O Jacob, you have not wearied yourselves for me, O Israel." Two lovers who never speak to each other are not two lovers. A husband who avoids his wife, who reads the paper when she wants to talk to him, who takes up hunting or reading to busy himself so that he won't have to commune with her, simply doesn't love her. Period.

The person who calls himself a Christian, who says he loves

God, yet does not seek his company and delight in it, can't be a true lover of God. His own flesh has deceived him. If he doesn't daily give his heart to God and receive God's heart in return, if he doesn't daily renew his hatred of his own sin and his delight in God's mercy, he has no relationship to God.

The flesh will pull countless tricks to get you away from your prayers and meditations. It will "reason" that you have to take care of your body before your spirit, because if your body dies you won't be of any use to God—so that you work so hard at earning money to make your family secure that you eventually have no time to talk with God. The flesh will get you to swap duties, so that you think that since you have family devotions or go to public worship, you don't need to be alone with God. It'll hoodwink you into making promises: "I'll pray to God next week, after I get past this big project at work." Of course, next week there is another big project at work—and there always will be something to take you away from God.

Listen to this and remember it always:

> What you are
> when you are alone with God,
> that you are—
> and nothing more.

You may make a great show of love and faith in church, singing like Pavarotti or attracting the masses to your profound Sunday school lectures. But if there is no private communion between you and Jesus—frequent and deep communion—then your religion is worthless. You've lost your first love. You stand at the end of Jesus' finger, aimed at your face with his threat:

> You have forsaken your first love. Remember the height from which you have fallen! Repent and do the things you did at first. If you do not repent, I will come to you and remove your lampstand from its place. (Revelation 2:4–5)

Falling in Love Again

A threat or a warning is a kindness—when you heed it. If you are speeding along the highway, and you see a sign that says, "DANGER! BRIDGE OUT AHEAD! CHOOSE ALTERNATE ROUTE!" yet you keep barreling along, you will die. But if you pay attention, stop, turn around, you will live.

On the other side of Jesus' threat in Revelation 2 is a marvelous promise: If we renew our first love, Jesus says, "I will give [you] the right to eat from the tree of life, which is in the paradise of God" (verse 7). This tree of life is Jesus himself. Can you fathom what an unspeakable gift this is? Is there anything in you that hungers and thirsts to eat that fruit, to give your heart away to him and receive his holy heart in return?

Jesus is the Pearl of Great Price, for which you should sell everything to buy. Jesus is the Treasure hidden in a field. Jesus is your Defender and Advocate, who kneels before the Father to pray for you. Jesus is the Power of God and the Wisdom of God. Jesus is the Desired of the nations. Jesus is the Friend for sinners, the Lover of your soul. Jesus is the Rising Sun, the Star of the Morning. Jesus is the Radiance of God's glory. Jesus gives himself to all who love him with first-love fire.

The flesh brings an ocean against your love for Jesus. It would drown your love for Christ. Don't wait till you are treading water to defend yourself. Cut him off now. Murder the flesh.

> For if you live according to the sinful nature, you will die; but if by the Spirit you put to death the misdeeds of the body, you will live. . . . (Romans 8:13)

Questions for Reflection and Discussion

1. Remember the time when you loved Christ most—when your love for him burned hot. If you are in a group, describe that love to them.

2. First love is known by humility—the lover often thinks himself unworthy of his beloved's love. A lover of Jesus feels this in a sense of how he has hurt his beloved, yet been forgiven. That sense of unworthiness, when it by faith accepts Christ's love, makes us love him more. What are some ways you can renew your sense of wonder at how much you've been forgiven?

3. First love is known by its hunger for its beloved, and its loss of appetite for anything else. For a lover of Jesus, "The things of earth will grow strangely dim in the light of his glory and grace." How can you stim-

ulate your hunger for the things of God, and suppress your appetite for the things of the world? (Can you do one without the other?)

4. What can you do to keep your worship from becoming formal and outward?

5. What is the purpose of knowledge of the Scriptures? How can it feed the fires of love for Jesus?

6. Calling on the Spirit to search your heart, use the following questions to help determine whether you have forsaken your first love for Jesus.

   ■ Is your zeal for God as warm, living, vigorous, effective, and eager as it was when you first gave yourself to God?

   ■ Do rivers of tears still flow from your eyes when God is dishonored (Psalm 119:136)?

   ■ Do you contend as violently as you once did for the faith?

   ■ Do you concern yourself as much as you once did with the glory of God in the world?

   ■ Does your life judge the world by its holiness and separateness as it used to?

   ■ Is your faith growing stronger?

   ■ Do you delight in public worship as you did when you first came to Christ?

   ■ Do you find the same relish and sweetness you once found in worship?

   ■ Is the preaching of the Word as precious to you as it was?

   ■ Do you listen to the Word eagerly and respond in faith and repentance?

- Do you anticipate the Sabbath as a time of joyous fellowship, as a foretaste of heaven?
- Do you hunger for holy conversation with others?
- Are you as careful about obedience as you were in the past?
- Is your conscience as tender toward sin as it was?
- Are you as faithful in private prayer and meditation?
- Do you love your brothers and sisters more than before?
- Are you as ready for crosses and burdens and persecution?
- Are you as humble?
- Are you as willing to deny yourself for the sake of the Kingdom?

part four

Nailing the Lid on Sin's Coffin

The corpse of an enemy always smells sweet.
—Napoleon I

11 | *a bone-marrow transplant*

> *. . . I grew up*
> *Fostered alike by beauty and by fear.*
> —William Wordsworth

To the Brink of Death

A bone-marrow transplant can make you wish you were dead.

When cancer gets into the marrow, a doctor has to all but kill his patient in order to save him. He destroys the bone marrow with radiation, then replaces it with healthy marrow to get it growing again. If the patient survives, he has a long and hard road back from the brink of death. But he is healed.

Seeing God can make you wish you were dead.

When Isaiah saw God on his throne in the temple, the prophet was ruined (Isaiah 1–6). When Job was filled with pride, God loved him and blasted him with his glory from the storm, till Job fell apart: "I despise myself and repent in dust and ashes" (Job 42:5–6). When Habakkuk saw a vision of God's power, he felt the sickness in his marrow.

I heard and my heart pounded,
  my lips quivered at the sound;
decay crept into my bones,
  and my legs trembled. (Habakkuk 3:16)

God's terrible majesty is radiation. It X-rays a soul and shows that it's gorged with sin. The soul sees what God is like in his glory, sees what it is like in its sickness, and buries its face in the dirt. Then the healing starts. God's radiating majesty kills the rotten marrow of sin and replaces it with humility. A heart humbled by God's terrible majesty can begin its recovery and grow strong. Sin can't thrive in a humble heart.

A vision of God like Isaiah's or Job's or Habakkuk's can't be made to order. But if we want to put sin to death in our hearts, we have to swallow the strongest doses of God's terrible majesty we can. We find them in our meditations on the Word.

The Medicine of Humiliation

Think greatly of God's greatness. Thoughts that reach up toward the excellency of God's majesty are beautiful and delicious to the soul, but they come with unpleasant side effects. Even a hint of his greatness shows us up as grasshoppers, dust, and "less than nothing" in comparison (Isaiah 40:12–25). No one wants to go out of his way to feel small, weak, and defiled; but this strong medicine gives us hope against sin. In this humiliation our sin withers.

We have a helpful problem in thinking of God's greatness: we can't do it! He is too much. Our puny minds can't take him in. And that helps, because it humbles us before him. Think of how little you know God. Can you walk up to the edge of infinity and not feel vertigo? Can you stare at the sun and not go blind? Agur must have felt that trying to know God's glory was like trying to understand the Atlantic by staring at a drop of its water:

> I am the most ignorant of men;
>> I do not have a man's understanding.
> I have not learned wisdom,
>> nor have I knowledge of the Holy One.
> Who has gone up to heaven and come down?
>> Who has gathered up the wind in the hol-
>> low of his hands?
> Who has wrapped up the waters in his cloak?
>> Who has established all the ends of the
>> earth?
> What is his name, and the name of his son?
>> Tell me if you know! (Proverbs 30:2–4)

But don't we see God more clearly now that he has come in the flesh? True, in the new covenant, the veil has been taken away so that we can see the glory of God in the face of Christ (2 Corinthians 4:6). But the sight we have of him, compared to what he is in himself, is dark and imperfect. Paul says it's like looking at God's reflection in a mirror.[1] Think of your face reflected in the hood of your car, not in the bathroom mirror, because a mirror to Paul was primitive, probably a sheet of polished brass. The way we see God now can't compare to the way we will see him when we are glorified: "When he appears . . . we shall see him as he is" (1 John 3:2).

Why do we know so little of him?

1. We know so little of him because he is God. He often describes himself by telling us what we can't know of him. We can't see him, we can't comprehend him, because he isn't like a man. In fact, there's no one like him.[2] And what we do know of him, we can't comprehend. We can only believe and admire. We say and believe that he is infinite and eternal, that he is everywhere and never changes, that he is three persons in one nature and the second person is two natures in one person. These ideas don't stretch the mind; they snap it.

We comprehend God as well as a six year old comprehends Einstein's theory of relativity.

2. We know so little of God because we only know him by faith. Faith is all the evidence we have of this invisible God (Hebrews 11:1). It is the only way we can come to him (verse 6). Our whole relationship with him in this life is summed up as walking by faith (2 Corinthians 5:7). We simply trust what he says about himself—that's how we know him.

But our knowledge of him by faith is just what we need in order to kill sin. We know him little, but we know him *truly*— enough to love him more than we do, delight in him and serve him more than we do, obey and trust him more than we do. We know him gloriously more than those did who knew him before Jesus came (Hebrews 1:1–3). We know him by the Spirit who lives in us. And to know him is to adore him.

Awe-full Worship Is the Death of Sin

Worship that God accepts is filled with reverence and awe that comes from considering who it is we worship, so that we are "fostered alike by beauty and by fear." We worship a tender Father as well as a "consuming fire" (Hebrews 12:28–29). Sin can't breathe in an atmosphere of fear and reverence before God. It suffocates. Can you imagine your lust cheery and prosperous when you are on your face before a holy God?

Questions for Reflection and Discussion

1. Think of a time when you felt overwhelmed by a sense of God's greatness, glory, and majesty. How did it happen? How did it affect your sin?
2. Do you work hard to get a glimpse of the glory of God each day as you approach him, or even each Sunday in worship? If so, how do you do it? If not, should you? How would you go about it?
3. Is it possible to see the glory of God in ordinary, everyday things (such as washing the car, changing a diaper, or finishing the third draft of a research paper)? Describe how it could happen.
4. The Scriptures are our only infallible guide for filling our minds and hearts with thoughts of God.

Choose a passage that zooms in on God (such as Isaiah 40:12–25; Job 38–41; or Psalm 68), and meditate on it till you find God great in your eyes and yourself small. If you meet with a group, talk about how well you did or didn't do at this.

12 | *no easy peace*

I believe it is peace for our time
. . . peace with honour.
—Neville Chamberlain

A Fool's Peace

When prime minister Neville Chamberlain returned to Britain from his meeting with Hitler in Munich, he waved before the crowd the agreement he had made with the Nazi leader and announced, "I believe it is peace for our time." Hitler had to roll over Czechoslovakia before Chamberlain gave up his wishful thinking. How much death and destruction might have been avoided if the prime minister had been more discerning about his enemy?

Chamberlain's declaration became an obscene irony when England went to war less than a year later. But as tragic as it was, men and women outdo his folly day after day, to the danger of their own souls. When their consciences are pricked by their own sin, they too quickly declare their own inner peace before God has done his work in them. Though they bless themselves, they lose

God's blessing and strengthen the flesh's foothold in them.

The God of Peace

It is God's sovereign prerogative to give his grace to whom he pleases (Romans 9:18). Even with those he has chosen to call and justify and purify, he reserves the privilege to declare peace to their conscience. He is the "God of all comfort" (2 Corinthians 1:3) who gives consolation to his children when and how he pleases. He alone creates peace for his people who sin.

> For this is what the high and lofty One says—
>> he who lives forever, whose name is holy:
> "I live in a high and holy place,
>> but also with him who is contrite and lowly
>>> in spirit,
> to revive the spirit of the lowly
>> and to revive the heart of the contrite.
> I will not accuse forever,
>> nor will I always be angry,
> for then the spirit of man would grow faint
>> before me—
>> the breath of man that I have created.
> I was enraged by his sinful greed;
>> I punished him, and hid my face in anger,
>> yet he kept on in his willful ways.
> I have seen his ways, but I will heal him;
>> I will guide him and restore comfort to him,

> creating praise on the lips of the mourners
>   in Israel.
> Peace, peace, to those far and near,"
>   says the LORD. "And I will heal them."
>   (Isaiah 57:15–19)

When God *creates* peace for whom he pleases, it is Christ's privilege to *declare* that peace. He is the "faithful and true witness" (Revelation 3:14) who shows us the condition of our souls. His judgment is righteous; his judgment alone can be trusted.

The Flesh's Peace

Hitler must have laughed all the way back to Berlin when he heard of Chamberlain's announcement. Your flesh is just as delighted when you accept its comfort rather than God's. Remember that the flesh is a con man, and it will do anything to keep you from killing it. One of its best cons is to make you believe that God is soothing your wounded conscience, so that you ease off your battle against sin.

You've got to learn how to discern between the comfort of God and the easy peace of the flesh. Here are some distinguishing marks:

1. You know it's your flesh talking when the peace comes and you don't yet abhor the sin. You know that the only remedy for your sin is the mercy of God through the blood of Christ. So when you are wounded by sin and feel the alienation from God and his people, you look to him for healing and quiet your heart: "Everything will be fine. Christ died for my sins. All is forgiven. Praise God!" But if with this your heart doesn't swell with hatred of the sin that wounded you, the words of peace are your own and not God's.

Our faith can look to Christ in different ways, depending on the occasion. By faith we sometimes see his holiness, sometimes his power, sometimes his love. When we come to Christ for healing and peace, we look to him as the One who was pierced, because "the punishment that brought us peace was upon him, and by his wounds we are healed" (Isaiah 53:5). When we see our bleeding Savior, we mourn and grieve (Zechariah 12:10) because it was our sin that pierced him. It is only his punishment that gives us peace, so when we look to him for peace, we must remember his pain. And we will detest our sin.[1]

Detesting sin is not the same as dreading the consequences of it. When you detest sin, you see it the way God does—how defiling it is. When you dabble in the things of the world, for example, your heart takes hold of God's judgment that "if anyone loves the world, the love of the Father is not in him" (1 John 2:15), and your heart weeps with self-hatred. *Then* God consoles you with his mercy in Christ.

2. You know it's your flesh talking when peace comes only by logic. It's possible, without the work of the Spirit, to use naked reasoning to apply Scriptures to soothe your conscience. In your tormented conscience you could turn to Isaiah 55:7 and read,

> Let the wicked forsake his way
>> and the evil man his thoughts.
> Let him turn to the LORD, and he will have
>> mercy on him,
>> and to our God, for he will freely pardon.

You could then reason, "In my mind I have turned from my sin; therefore, based on this promise, God has freely pardoned me." If you stumbled again into the sin and felt even more troubled over your backsliding, you could turn to Hosea 14:4 and read,

> I will heal their waywardness
>> and love them freely,
>> for my anger has turned away from them.

You could conclude that God is speaking to you in this verse and has turned his anger away from you. And having done this, you could be dead wrong. The words of peace could be spoken from the flesh with none of God in them.

"But wait a minute," you object. "This is the way the Spirit speaks, using his holy Word to refresh and heal us. How can I know when I'm just talking to myself?" Good question.

For one thing, if you are God's child, he will not let you wander far in a delusion (Psalm 25:9). The peace you give yourself won't last long. Another way to tell the difference is that "reasoned peace" comes quickly, but God over and over in his Word tells us to wait on him.

I will wait for the LORD,
> who is hiding his face from the house of
> Jacob.
I will put my trust in him. (Isaiah 8:17)

Self-healers are usually in a hurry, and can't wait on the Lord. Another difference is that "reasoned peace" doesn't give sweetness and contentment to the soul. When God speaks there is not only bare truth that satisfies the mind, but a power that settles the affections.

But the worst difference is that "reasoned peace" doesn't change your life. When God declares peace, he turns his people away from their sin.

> I will listen to what God the LORD will say;
>> he promises peace to his people, his
>> saints—
> but let them not return to folly. (Psalm 85:8)

Because the sweetness of God's love comes with his peace, you find your sin slain by his tender mercy.

3. You know it's your flesh talking when you take peace lightly. How easy it is to treat sin and forgiveness as an everyday thing—and yet how dangerous.

> They dress the wound of my people
>> as though it were not serious.
> "Peace, peace," they say,
>> when there is no peace. (Jeremiah 6:14)

"Just a glance of faith is all it takes," the flesh says. "Just a look over the shoulder at a few precious promises, and all is well." But the Word of God is worthless to your conscience if you don't look intently into it with *faith* (Hebrews 4:2). If you shop for peace with God the way you get dinner at McDonald's, you'll just as quickly find that it isn't true peace. Your sin will overwhelm you again before you know it.

4. You know it's your flesh talking when peace is selective. If you humble yourself before God and seek his healing peace about your stealing from your employer by playing games on your computer all day at work, yet don't seek his peace about your hot temper with your children, any peace you find will be clouds in your coffee.

The Peace of God

"My sheep know my voice" (John 10:4). Christ's faithful lambs know his voice because they are used to the sound of it. Because they commune with him often and hunger for the words that fall from his lips, they recognize the tone and rhythm of his precious words. They can tell at once whether he or a stranger is declaring peace. They know his voice because it speaks good to their souls. His word of peace humbles souls, cleanses from guilt, transforms lives, melts their hearts, and endears Christ to them.

When you hear Christ speaking peace to your soul, you can rest in his comfort. But your flesh will grow sickly and pale, drained of its power by a renewed taste of God's mercy in Christ's blood.

Questions for Reflection and Discussion

1. What makes your soul susceptible to the false peace the flesh offers?

2. What is the danger of accepting a false peace?

3. Of all the ways the flesh tries to get you to rest in a false peace, which are you most likely to accept? What makes it appealing to you?

4. Thinking back on what you have learned about your flesh, what is it about God's peace that delivers a mortal blow to the flesh?

5. This question goes beyond the realm of this book, but what are some ways the world tries to declare peace to your soul?

6. Have you given yourself false peace? How? How has it affected your relationship to God? To others?

13 | *lethal faith*

No coward soul is mine,
No trembler in the world's storm-troubled sphere:
I see Heaven's glories shine,
And faith shines equal, arming me from fear.
—Emily Brontë

Super Faith

Faster than a speeding bullet, more powerful than a locomotive, able to leap tall buildings in a single bound—Superman seems invincible. But if you can sneak a pebble of Kryptonite into his boot, he'll crumble in a heap of blue and red.

All the greatest heroes and villains of fables have their Achilles' heels. In Homer's *Iliad*, Achilles was unbeatable till Paris shot him in the heel, his only weak spot. The Wolfman will ravage the village every full moon—unless someone shoots him with a silver bullet. Count Dracula will drain Transylvania of its life—unless you can find him asleep in his coffin and pound a wooden stake through his heart.

Throughout this book I've mentioned many ways to fight against the flesh, such as

- meditating on the cross to see the rottenness of your sin and the fulness of Christ's love,
- keeping watch against sin's deceit,
- filling your affections with heavenly things,
- applying your will to every means of God's grace to fight temptation,
- renewing your first love for Jesus,
- hungering for a glimpse of God's holy glory.

But all these are mere preparation for the ultimate work of killing the flesh. They help steady the mind, rein in the affections, and discipline the will. Yet they will not destroy the flesh's work—unless, that is, they are combined with *faith*. Faith is Kryptonite, a wooden stake, and a silver bullet all in one.

Faith has to be the only thing that destroys the flesh because "salvation comes from the LORD" (Jonah 2:9). Faith has to be the only thing that destroys the flesh because the whole work of our salvation is God's from beginning to end. It isn't simply that God accepts us in Christ when we believe, then sends us off to be good little Christians on our own. Our growth in holiness is his work too (Philippians 2:13). The good news of Jesus is not just that we get out of hell free, but that we become like Jesus himself and are made able to live and reign with him forever in the new heaven and the new earth. And this good news is all "by faith from first to last," from beginning to end, through and through (Romans 1:17).

Siccing Christ on Your Sin

Jesus' blood alone can deliver from sin. Live in his blood and you will die a conqueror—you will, by the good providence of God, live to see your lust dead at your feet. Here's how to work your faith:

1. By faith fill your soul with thoughts of the purpose of Christ's death. Jesus died to slay the very lust that entangles you. In fact, it has you trapped precisely because you're no match for it. You may be worn and exhausted from the grief and shame of it, ready to throw up your hands and surrender to a life of sin. But there is stored up in Christ plenty of strength to relieve you (Philippians 4:13). In your deepest distress and anguish, consider the fulness of grace, the riches, the treasures of strength, might, and help that are stored in him for your help (John 1:16; Colossians 1:19). Remember that "God exalted him to his own right hand as Prince and Savior that he might give repentance and forgiveness of sins to Israel" (Acts 5:31). And if he gives repentance, then he puts to death the flesh, because there can't be repentance without striking a blow to the flesh. Working faith in Christ this way is how we remain in him and find his cleansing power (John 15:3; Romans 11:20).

To work faith in Christ's power over your flesh, your thoughts might run this way:

I am a poor, weak creature, unstable as water. I can't conquer my flesh. My corruption is too much for me and is a step away from ruining me. I don't know what to do. My soul is a desert, a cave full of dragons. I've made promises and broken them. Many times I thought I'd won and would be delivered, but I was deceived. I can tell that if I don't get some help right away, I'll give up on God and make a shipwreck of my faith.

But here at death's door I raise my weak arms. I look to you, Lord Christ, with all grace in your heart, all power in your hand, more than able to slay all my enemies. You can make me more than a conqueror. Why do you say, O my soul, that "my way is hidden from the LORD. . . . Do you not know? Have you not heard? The LORD is the everlasting God, the Creator of the ends of the earth. He will not grow tired or weary, and his understanding no one can fathom. He gives strength to the weary and increases the power of the weak. Even youths grow tired and weary, and young men stumble and fall; but those who hope in the LORD will renew their strength. They will soar on wings like eagles; they will run and not grow weary, they will walk and not be faint."[1]

If these are your thoughts, you will find that his grace is sufficient for you (2 Corinthians 12:9).

2. By faith expect help to come from Christ. "Though it linger, wait for it; it will certainly come and will not delay" (Habakkuk 2:3). It may seem a long time in coming, because of your trouble and perplexity; yet it will come from Jesus. It will come in his time, which is the best time. "As the eyes of slaves look to the hand of their master, as the eyes of a maid look to the hand of her mistress," let your eyes look to Christ for help (Psalm 123:2). Trust him to deliver as he has promised, and he will come to slay your lust and give you peace. But

> if you do not stand firm in your faith,
>> you will not stand at all. (Isaiah 7:9)

If you ask what foundation you have to build your expectations on, remember that you have no other options. To whom will you go? Christ alone has the words of life (John 6:68). Without him you can do nothing (John 15:5). Your only strength comes from Christ dwelling in your heart by faith (Ephesians 3:16–17). You can only put the misdeeds of the flesh to death "by the Spirit" (Romans 8:13). And who sends and commands the Spirit but Christ?

You want more reason to expect Christ's help? Think about his mercy, tenderness, and kindness as your High Priest at the right hand of God.

> For this reason he had to be made like his brothers in every way, in order that he might become a merciful and faithful high priest in service to God, and that he might make atonement for the sins of the people. Because he himself suffered when he was tempted, he is able to help those who are being tempted. (Hebrews 2:17–18)

> For we do not have a high priest who is unable to sympathize with our weaknesses, but we have one who has been tempted in every way, just as we are—yet was with-

out sin. Let us then approach the throne of grace with confidence, so that we may receive mercy and find grace to help us in our time of need. (Hebrews 4:15–16)

Do you need something more to bolster your hope of deliverance? Think about the *faithfulness* of the one who promised to help you. Because the psalmist knew the certainty of his Lord's covenant, he could wait for help from him "more than watchmen wait for the morning" (Psalm 130:6). Christ's help comes as surely as the sun will rise in the morning—in its appointed time.

3. Set your faith particularly on Christ's death, blood, and cross—that is, on Jesus as the slain Lamb. The death of sin comes through the death of Christ. He died to destroy the flesh. Whatever temptations wail away at you each day, Christ died to destroy them all.

[He] gave himself for us to redeem us from all wickedness and to purify for himself a people that are his very own, eager to do what is good. (Titus 2:14)

His design was to free us from the power of sin. He gave himself for the church to cleanse it and purge from it every blemish (Ephesians 5:25–27), and his death will fully accomplish this. The Scriptures always attribute our cleaning and purifying to his blood (1 John 1:7; Hebrews 1:3; 9:14; Revelation 1:5). It is our union with him in his death that makes us dead to sin, so that we can't live in sin any longer (Romans 6:1–14)—so that "we too may live a new life" (verse 4).

Look to Christ's death for power. Look to his death in order to become like him and die to sin. Look on him groaning under the weight of your sins, praying, bleeding, and dying for you. Apply his blood to your filth. *Do this every day.*

By My Spirit, Says the Lord

In your struggle against sin, never forget your duty—but neither forget the power of the Spirit. The killing of the flesh is your duty, but his work.

> If *by the Spirit* you put to death the misdeeds of the body, you will live. (Romans 8:13)

As you by faith apply all the means of grace God has given to kill the flesh, remember that it is the Spirit who works in every part to bring the victory from Christ.

1. The Spirit alone convinces your heart of the danger of sin. You won't take up the means of grace and look to the cross till lust's threat grabs you by the throat—that is, till the Spirit grabs you. He convinces of sin (John 16:8). If any rational mind could do the work by itself when it heard the Word of God, we'd see a lot more weeping for sin than we do. Without the Spirit's conviction, the flesh will thrive.

2. The Spirit alone reveals and teaches the fulness of Christ for your deliverance. This is what keeps us from becoming despondent in the battle.

None of the rulers of this age understood it, for if they had, they would not have crucified the Lord of glory. However, as it is written:

"No eye has seen,
>   no ear has heard,
> no mind has conceived
>>   what God has prepared for those who love
>>   him"—

but God has revealed it to us by his Spirit. (1 Corinthians 2:8–10)

3. The Spirit alone settles your heart in expectation of help from Christ. This is God's sovereign means of killing your flesh.

Now it is God who makes both us and you stand firm in Christ. He anointed us, set his seal of ownership on us, and put his Spirit in our hearts as a deposit, guaranteeing what is to come. (2 Corinthians 1:21–22)

4. The Spirit alone fixes the cross in your heart with its sin-killing power. By the Spirit we are baptized into Christ's death.

5. The Spirit is the Author and Finisher of our sanctification. He gives us new shipments of grace for holiness (Ephesians 3:16–19).

6. The Spirit alone supports us when we cry out to God in distress over sin. Many people talk about the power of prayer as if our words or will could move God. The Scriptures say the *Spirit* is the real power of prayer, giving life, vigor, and strength to our prayer, and making it persuasive to God. When we can't drag ourselves out of bed, he enables us to pray with "groans that words cannot express" (Romans 8:26).

Happy Thanksgiving!

You will win. You will fight, and you will see your flesh crumble. It is God's pleasure not only to rescue you from hell, but to glorify you with Christ by making you like him. You will see through your flesh's most deadly deception. You will turn your eyes away from its most appealing idols. And you will grow in self-discipline and courage.

But this is no time to puff out your chest. It's Christ's blood, tenderness, and mercy on you. It's his Spirit's power filling you every step of the way. In every victory lift your hands to heaven and give thanks—rejoice with a grateful heart in your Deliverer. He is faithful.

Soli Deo gloria.

Questions for Reflection and Discussion

1. What are some ways people try to break sin's power without faith and the Spirit of God? What is it about faith that makes it such a powerful weapon against the flesh?

2. Suppose someone you love is depending on you for help. How does that motivate you? Or suppose the same person needs your help, but refuses to depend on you, even doubts that you're willing to help. How does that motivate you? Now apply that to Jesus. How does your expectation of help from him move him to help you?

3. Reread Hebrews 2:17–18 and 4:15–16. Christ, as Lord, never lacked the power to atone for our sins. Why, then, did he *have* to be made like his brothers in every way? In what sense did becoming like us enable him to be our High Priest?

4. Look back to the prayer you wrote for chapter 1, question 7. What has God taught you through this study? Did he answer your prayers? Write a prayer of thanksgiving to him. But the work isn't finished—so write another prayer for his power and your perseverance in the war against *the enemy within.*

notes

Preface

1 *A Quest for Godliness: The Puritan Vision of the Christian Life* (Wheaton: Crossway, 1990); *Rediscovering Holiness* (Ann Arbor: Vine, 1992); *Keep in Step with the Spirit* (Old Tappan, N.J.: Revell, 1984).

2 John Owen, *Works,* ed. William Goold (Edinburgh: Johnstone and Hunter, 1850–53). Both *Indwelling Sin* and *The Mortification of Sin* are in volume 6. Sixteen of the volumes of Goold's edition were reprinted photographically by The Banner of Truth Trust, 1965–68.

3 I particularly appreciate and recommend R. J. K. Law's *The Glory of Christ* (Edinburgh: Banner, 1994) and *Communion with God* (Edinburgh: Banner, 1991).

Part One: The Power of Sin in What It Is

Chapter 1: Evil at My Elbow

1 Romans 7 has been variously interpreted; but on close inspection it is clearly describing the experience of a believer, rather than an unbeliever. For a brief but clear discussion of this, see J. I. Packer, *Keep in Step with the Spirit* (Old Tappan, N.J.: Revell, 1984), 263–70. See also John R. W. Stott, *Men Made New: An Exposition of Romans 5–8* (1966; American ed. Grand Rapids: Baker, 1984), 71–75.

2 Throughout this book I will use these terms interchangeably.

3 There are two other enemies: the world and the Devil. I will not deal with them explicitly. But since they both do their dirty work by appealing to our flesh (indwelling sin), any victory over the flesh will work to weaken them as well.

4 Think of your sanctification in terms of Christ's coming to earth. In his first coming he inaugurated his kingdom in the world: he is already ruling and reigning, he has defeated the god of this age, he is seated on his throne at the right hand of the Father; yet the opposition remains, the battle continues. In his second coming he will consummate his kingdom, ridding it from every enemy. Being born again is the first coming of Christ to your soul: he truly rules and reigns in your heart, but the defeated enemy remains and the battle continues. Your glorification after death is the second coming of Christ to your soul, when every last trace of the law of sin will be disintegrated.

5 Though grace ordinarily prevails in us, in this life it never does so perfectly (Galatians 5:17). Even in our most loving, humble moments, a touch of pride slips in to tarnish our most righteous works. We ever live absolutely dependent on Christ.

John described the heart of the believer renewed by Christ and under his rule: "No one who is born of God will continue to sin, because God's seed remains in him; he cannot go on sinning, because he has been born of God" (1 John 3:9). To "continue to sin" and to "go on sinning" mean to make sin your career in life. The believer has a new nature—the seed of God in him—that cannot live at peace with sin. This distinguishes believers at their *worst* from unbelievers at their *best*. Even when the believer stumbles and seems most to be bullied by the tyrant sin, his new heart is still hating sin, so that he has no peace until it is crushed. But an unbeliever who appears on the surface to be kind and respectable will, if God removes his restraining grace from him, willingly and with relish give himself to sin.

6 Remember Rehoboam? See 1 Kings 12.

Chapter 2: The Long Arm of the Law

1 See, for example, Matthew 5:10–12; 24:9; John 16:33; Philippians 1:29; 2 Timothy 1:8; 3:12; 1 Peter 4:12; Revelation 2:10.

2 See chapters 11–13 for a display of the hard work needed to put sin to death.

3 *Inferno,* Canto 34.

Chapter 3: The Haunted House

1 The word "affections" is an old one, but we need to keep it. "Emotions" is too small to capture all that the old word meant. Affections include emotions, longings, revulsion, imagination, and more.

2 For a fair and careful critique of different views of sanctification, see J. I. Packer, *Keep in Step with the Spirit,* 121–69.

Chapter 4: Irreconcilable Differences

1 Many translations render the sense of Romans 8:7 as ". . . the sinful mind is hostile to God" (NIV). The stricter reading of the KJV and NKJV preserve the nuance that is the point of this chapter.

2 In Ephesians 2:14–16 Christ brings two other enemies together, Jew and Gentile, again by putting to death the hostility that was between them.

3 I'm not against looking for new insights from Scripture, listening to music just for fun, or giving presents to friends. The point is that the more spiritual something is—the more likely it is to bring us to close communion with God—the more strenuously the flesh will resist it.

Part Two: The Power of Sin in How It Works

Chapter 5: The Tricks of the Trade

1 Mark Twain, *Adventures of Huckleberry Finn,* chapter 20.

2 Ibid.

3 See, for example, Luke 21:8; 1 Corinthians 6:9; 15:33; Galatians 6:7; Ephesians 5:6.

4 If you watch your own heart carefully, you'll find that these three faculties don't always work as a team. The fall has thrown them out of harmony. Sometimes the affections can't get excited about what the mind knows is good (such as worshiping in the sanctuary when the sun is shining on the golf course); or the will seems powerless to fall in behind the mind and affections (as when you know you should love God with all your heart, and you want to, but just can't). Still, the mind is designed to be the watchman, and deceit is aimed right at him.

5 Compare Matthew 6:22–23: "The eye is the lamp of the body. If your eyes are good, your whole body will be full of light. But if your eyes are bad, your whole body will be full of darkness. If then the light within you is darkness, how great is that darkness!"

6 Compare Proverbs 7:21–27. The adulterous woman is representative not only of sexual sin but of all sin.

7 I mean, of course, *wicked* used-car salesmen. There are honest men and women who sell used cars.

8 God aborts conceived sin by his providence in many ways. For example, a man may lust for a woman and determine in his heart to seduce her, but she is unwilling. The man still sinned (with mind, affections, and will), but was powerless to carry out the action. Though Owen discusses this at length, I have omitted it from this book. See Owen, *Indwelling Sin,* chapter 13.

Chapter 6: Getting Carried Away

1 See chapter 2, the discussion of the rewards and punishments of sin.

2 For a useful (lengthy) meditation on this, see the Puritan Edward Reynolds, *The Sinfulness of Sin* (Reprint. Ligonier, Pa.: Soli Deo Gloria, 1992).

3 Ephesians 5:10.

Chapter 7: No Idle Mind

1 The Psalms and songs of praise in the Bible are your best guide for this kind of meditation.

2 See 1 Corinthians 2:6–16.

3 See Romans 8:26–27.

4 Of course life isn't cut and dried. There are seasons when your work rightly needs more time than usual, times when your family needs extraordinary attention—and times when your prayers have to push everything else aside.

Chapter 8: Hooked

1 The writers of Proverbs expose the deceits of the flesh like those who know what they're talking about. Listen to them.

2 Augustine, *The Confessions* 6.15.

3 Dear Paula, I *will* get you that sewing cabinet—someday!

4 Look at the lives of Samson, Solomon, and David.

5 See 2 Peter 2:14. Those whose eyes (imaginations, fantasies) are full of adultery "never stop sinning."

6 See Romans 12:11.

7 Izaak Walton, *The Compleat Angler.*

Chapter 9: Maculate Conception

1 Look back at James 1:14–15 to see the pattern of the deceit of sin, which we have been tracing since chapter 5.

2 Owen explores the "abortion" of conceived sin at length in chapter 13 of *Indwelling Sin.* The basic idea is that God often puts an end to sin before it is carried out. A man may determine in his heart to rob a bank, but never have the opportunity or means. But note that there is nothing lacking in his soul to make the thwarted robbery a sin: his mind somehow thought the robbery good to commit, the affections wanted to get the money, and the will gave it his best shot. From God's perspective the man is a thief. This partly explains why Jesus could say

that a man who lusts after a woman has already committed adultery in his heart (Matthew 5:28): not because "thinking about a sin" is as bad as doing it, but because his mind, affections, and will have already done all they can do to sin.

3 Compare and consider Victor Hugo's description of Jean Valjean who, after being "redeemed" by the Bishop of Digne, stole a coin from poor little Gervais:

> Let us say simply, it was not he who robbed, it was not the man, but the brute beast that through habit and instinct stupidly placed its foot on the coin, while the intellect was struggling with such novel and extraordinary sensations. When the intellect woke again and saw this brutish action, Jean Valjean recoiled with agony and uttered a cry of horror. It was a curious phenomenon, and one only possible in the situation he was in, that, in robbing the boy of that money, he committed a deed of which he was no longer capable (*Les Miserables*, 1.2.13).

4 For a detailed discussion of the will, see Jonathan Edwards, *Freedom of the Will*, especially part 1, section 2.

5 Protestants often scoff at the Roman Catholic idea of annulment, assuming it is motivated by this sort of thinking. But what some Catholics are persuaded by the flesh to do with official sanction, thousands of Protestants accomplish without a pope's blessing.

Part Three: The Power of Sin in What It Does

Chapter 10: Slip-Sliding Away

1 See Jeremiah 2:2–3; 1 Timothy 5:12; Hebrews 3:14; 2 John 8.

2 Consider, for example, that five of the seven churches that Jesus addresses in Revelation 2–3 he charges with spiritual decay—Revelation 2:4–5, 14–16, 20–21; 3:1–3, 15–18.

3 Read Psalm 50 to see God calling his people to account for their empty worship—and tremble before God when you pre-

tend to come into his presence, sauntering in after the worship has begun, your thoughts and desires ten thousand miles away from him. Think of his fire burning when you ignore his voice in the preaching of the Word, and listen to sermon after sermon without even giving a single thought to your sin or his beauty.

4 See Augustine's *Confessions* 6.15 and 8.7.

5 Read Ezekiel 33:32 for a striking example of this.

Part Four: Nailing the Lid on Sin's Coffin

Chapter 11: A Bone-Marrow Transplant

1 First Corinthians 13:12; 2 Corinthians 3:18. The word in 2 Corinthians 3:18 translated "reflect" in the NIV is better translated by the footnote, "contemplate." It means to look at something as it is reflected in a mirror. Compare the NASB, KJV, NKJV, RSV, NRSV, REB, and commentaries.

2 Exodus 8:10; 15:11; Numbers 23:19; Job 28; Psalm 77:13; Isaiah 40:12–25; 46:5; Hosea 11:9; Romans 11:33–36; 1 Corinthians 2:16; Colossians 1:15; 1 Timothy 1:17; 6:16.

Chapter 12: No Easy Peace

1 See Ezekiel 16:59–63.

Chapter 13: Lethal Faith

1 Isaiah 40:28–31.

OTHER TITLES OF INTEREST:

Addictions—A Banquet in the Grave: Finding Hope in the Power of the Gospel (978-0-87552-606-5) by Edward T. Welch

Growing Up Christian (978-0-87552-611-9) by Karl Graustein with Mark Jacobsen

Idols of the Heart: Learning to Long for God Alone (978-0-87552-198-5) by Elyse Fitzpatrick

Instruments in the Redeemer's Hands: People in Need of Change Helping People in Need of Change (978-0-87552-607-2) by Paul David Tripp

Pleasing People: How Not to be an "Approval Junkie" (978-1-59638-055-4) by Lou Priolo

When People Are Big and God Is Small: Overcoming Peer Pressure, Codependency, and the Fear of Man (978-0-87552-600-3) by Edward T. Welch

For more information on these and other titles, please visit our website:

WWW.PRPBOOKS.COM